The Appalachian Dulcimer Book

The Appalachian Dulcimer Book

Drawn by F. R. Gruger

Illustration from a 1912 *Century Magazine*

Half-tone plate engraved by R. C. Collins

by Michael Murphy

music transcribed
by Denny Kleinman

FOLKSAY PRESS

REVISED

Second Printing

Copyright © 1976, by Michael Murphy

All Rights Reserved

You may order single copies prepaid direct from the publisher for $4.95 + .50 per copy postage and handling (including sales tax)

Published by:
FOLKSAY PRESS
Mills Road, R. R. 3
St. Clairsville, Ohio 43950

Distributed to the music trade by:
MUSIC SALES INC.
33 West 60th St.
New York, N. Y. 10023

Distributed to the book trade by:
BOOKPEOPLE
2940 Seventh St.
Berkeley, California, 94710

Library of Congress Card Catalog Number
75-35427

I. S. B. N.
0-916454-01-0

Printed in the United States of America

Photographic Credits

Front cover photograph by Doris Ulmann, courtesy University of Oregon Library

Photographs by Doris Ulmann, courtesy University of Oregon Library
    Pages: 23, 45, 60, 63, 77, 83, 86

Photographs courtesy Nordiska Museet
    Page: 21

Photographs courtesy Smithsonian Institution
    Pages: 26, 27, 28, 29, 30

Photographs courtesy Metropolitan Museum of Art, The Crosby Brown Collection of Musical Instruments, 1889
    Pages: 20, 23

Photographs courtesy William Barnhill
    Pages: 13, 15, 18

Photograph courtesy Norsk Folkemuseum
    Page: 22

Photograph courtesy National Museum of Iceland
    Page: 23

Photograph courtesy Virginia Historical Society
    Page: 11

Photograph courtesy Bucks County Historical Society
    Page: 20

Photograph courtesy U.S. Forest Service
    Page: 12

Illustration from *The Century Magazine,* copyright 1912
Reproduced by permission of Prentice-Hall Inc., Englewood Cliffs, New Jersey.
    Page: 3

Illustration courtesy *Harpers Magazine*
    Pages: 9, 35, 93

Photograph courtesy Levi Jackson State Park, Kentucky
    Page: 31

Photographs courtesy University of Louisville
    Pages: 32, 33, 42, 51, 53, 55, 59, 66, 80, 89, 91

Photograph courtesy Library of Congress
    Page: 57

CONTENTS

THE INSTRUMENT AND ITS HISTORY

- 11 Appalachian Folk Music
- 12 Dulcimer Folklore
- 13 The Dulcimore (a story)
- 19 Origins of the Appalachian Dulcimer
- 25 Early Dulcimer Construction
- 32 Early Dulcimer Makers

MAKING MUSIC

- 37 Introduction to Playing
- 37 Modal Music
- 38 Tuning
- 40 Tuning Charts
- 43 Reading Music
- 47 Picks and Noters
- 48 Strumming
- 64 Bowing
- 64 Picking
- 70 Chord Formation
- 71 Using Chords
- 72 Chord Charts
- 76 Counter Melodies
- 88 Bending Notes
- 88 Hammering On
- 88 Tremolo
- 88 Pulling Off Notes
- 88 Harmonics
- 88 Triplets
- 89 Accompanying Other Instruments
- 90 Translating Printed Music

CONTENTS

SONGS FOR THE DULCIMER

75	Amazing Grace	Ionian Mode
87	Down In The Valley	Ionian Mode
54	Drill Ye Tarriers	Aeolian Mode
84	Greensleeves	Aeolian Mode
78	Hush Li'l Baby	Ionian Mode
58	John Henry	Mixolydian Mode
65	Long Long Ago	Ionian Mode
62	Old Dan Tucker	Ionian Mode
48	Old Gray Goose, The (First)	Ionian Mode
67	Old Gray Goose, The (Second)	Ionian Mode
74	Old Gray Goose, The (Third)	Ionian Mode
76	Old Gray Goose, The (Fourth)	Ionian Mode
79	Old Gray Goose, The (Fifth)	Ionian Mode
56	Old Joe Clark	Mixolydian Mode
52	Pretty Polly	Dorian Mode
61	Scarborough Fair	Dorian Mode
81	Shenandoah	Ionian Mode
68	Sumer Is Icumen In	Ionian Mode
49	Sweet Betsy From Pike	Ionian Mode
82	Tom Dooley	Ionian Mode

APPENDIX

- 94 Buying a Dulcimer
- 94 Dulcimer Repairs
- 96 Dulcimer Makers List
- 97 Sources for Buying Dulcimer Wood
- 97 Other Dulcimer Instruction Books
- 97 Dulcimer Construction Books
- 98 Bibliography
- 100 Discography
- 102 Record Company Addresses

THE INSTRUMENT AND ITS HISTORY

Illustration from a 1915 *Harpers Magazine*

Mountaineer's cabin at the turn of the century

Appalachian Folk Music

Folk music possesses many distinctive qualities. Most importantly, it is an expression of the character of the people. This character is conveyed in a folk song's melody and lyrics which have been passed on and refined through the years. Although folk song melodies do remain basically unaltered, their lyrics adapt to suit their environment and their cultural setting.

For this reason, songs that evolved in the Appalachians developed their own unique flavor. This is the result of both the harsh living conditions that existed in the mountains, and the heritage of the English and Scottish settlers who arrived there in the early seventeenth century. These immigrants, seeking to ease the transition of relocating in a new land, attempted to create a musical community corresponding to the one they had left in the Old World. The songs that the settlers carried with them that were suited to the mountains and to their emotional needs were retained.

Most of the songs transported from the Old World to the Appalachians were ballads, narrative songs with many stanzas. The majority of Appalachian ballads can be traced to sixteenth and seventeenth century England. There they had originated as broadsides, printed music on one side of a piece of paper, which were commercially written and distributed. In Britain ballads usually contained more than one hundred stanzas, although in the Appalachians British ballads were pared down greatly to blend in with the stark living conditions. These old ballads underwent many other modifications in their new land. The common man, of little importance in British ballads, made an emergence in the wilderness. Songs with English names were gradually altered, and supernatural and ritual songs, popular across the sea, served no function in the mountains and perished.

The lyrics that survived dealt with universal themes of romance, battle, adventure, and history. It is easy to understand why in this harsh setting the most prevalent song lyrics sung by men pertained to battle, adventure, and history. However, women were motivated to sing romantic songs for other reasons. Mountain women had little control over their personal lives. Guilt and repression were widespread, and these vengeful, romantic songs, thought so evil that they were never sung before

11

children, were directed at their frustrations.

Although a majority of the Appalachian music originated in England, mountain music was also shaped by the American Blacks. Many Blacks found their way into the mountains working on farms and railroad crews. They brought with them their native African banjo along with their own distinctive musical style. These Blacks descended from a culture that placed a high value on erotic behavior. Also, being second class citizens, they weren't expected to conform to the White's social conventions. This enabled them to retain their joyous and sensual song and dance ceremonies which were in vivid contrast to the typical English immigrants singing.

The Appalachian Highlander's music was also negatively influenced by religion. The Primitive Baptist Church, which gained momentum in the mountains in the early twentieth century, put musical instruments aside as the devil's work. These Baptists wouldn't even tolerate instrumental accompaniment for their religious songs.

Not long after this religious upsurge, the technological breakthroughs of the twentieth century destroyed the barriers of isolation that shielded the mountain songs from change for over three centuries. One of the largest bodies of American folk song, preserved by hundreds of years of isolation, then became accessible to the remainder of the country.

Dulcimer Folklore

Over the last few years the dulcimer, an ancient instrument played exclusively in the Appalachian Mountains, has been finding its way back into the mainstream of American folk music. However, not too long ago the likelihood of this occurring appeared highly remote. Josiah H. Combs, a folklorist who researched the Appalachian dulcimer's origins, wrote in 1925, "The dulcimer is an instrument formerly used but now falling rapidly into decay." How wrong he turned out to be, for the dulcimer remains one of the earliest American folk instruments still in common usage. Even though the oldest dulcimer remnants date back to the early 1800's, its history undoubtedly precedes this date.

Through the years "dulcimer" has been the most widely accepted name for this instrument, although it has also been known as a hog fiddle or scattlin. It was sometimes referred to as a scattlin, since this was the name given to two by fours, the material out of which some dulcimers were constructed in the early 1800's.

Several other assorted bits of folklore surround the dulcimer. One practice includes placing snake rattles in the instrument's body, supposedly making the strings really sing out. More likely, the dulcimer was considered more appropriate for

Mountaineer's cabin in North Carolina, 1901

The Dulcimore

The mounting summer had at last escaped the grasp of the April chill, and the season's growth came on with a headlong rush. The forest was one rustling loom of life-stuff, everywhere thrilling to a million-tinted glories of summer beauty and abundance. Between twin hills that lay against the sky, dark and softly rounded as the breasts of a slave-mother, the old smithy nestled. It was a log structure, low and windowless, and lighted like a grotto with blue and greenish reflections from the hot sunshine outside.

The young giant in the leather apron was clanking steadily on with his task, albeit he had a visitor. Straight from trysting with the wind among the blossoming laurel on the hill, she came into this place of grime and toil, with perfume yet on her garments, and her dreams in her eyes. Georgia Carden, daughter of old Jared Carden and his wife Selina, who lived on a good farm under which coal had been found in fairly profitable quantities, was a noted figure in her environment.

"She sha'n't go with the young folks around here," her mother said, half fiercely. "Let her roam as she will; the woods'll be all lumber and tan-bark soon enough; let her enjoy them while she can."

In the twenty years of her wifehood, which began with galling poverty, Selina Carden's pride had never faltered, yet she had not been so foolish as to prefer utter failure to makeshift. She adapted herself in order not to die, and she had so managed that all her children were actually rich. For each babe that came were the clean changes, constantly forthcoming on demand, that she could not afford for herself. For the new babe's sake she forbore cruel toil a while. Later, she furbished her early knowledge to set them in the way of permanent riches, by teaching them what she knew of their immediate world, supplementing the crude schooling which was all they could have, to fit them to enjoy a life which had never been hers. But the Carden lads, as they grew, would have none of such impalpable possessions. Georgia alone, on the opening of the coal veins beneath the farm, asked the reason for the dainty fern-prints in the shale. Her brothers echoed only chance-caught information about freight rates and comparative values. Was it strange that the girl, her youngest, seemed of all Selina's children

Taken near Asheville, North Carolina, 1915

a female player. These rattles probably enhanced the instrument's masculinity, making it acceptable for a hearty male mountaineer to play. Another practice, followed by some people who prized their dulcimers highly, was naming their daughters Dulcina which means sweet one. These and other bits of folklore which surround this instrument endow it with a particular quality.

To gain a better appreciation of the dulcimer and for the area where it was originally played, the story *The Dulcimore*, which first appeared in a 1909 *Harper's Magazine*, is reprinted here.

peculiarly her own—that the usual mother-dream of a relation to endure indefinitely was here intensified?

"Howdy, Return," the girl spoke from the doorway, her light lawn dress blowing about her, the sun at her back, facing the shadows. Her mother's indulgence had given her years of faerie wanderings and dreaming to remember; and now any day that dawned might hold ere sunset the hour of the Prince's coming, the morning of love, with music and white light. The consciousness of this imminence was aglow in her face as she flitted across the earthen floor and perched moth-like on the work-bench, where scraps and broken tools were piled in rusty confusion.

By way of welcome the young smith fetched her a drink of cool spring water in a dripping gourd. There was something about him that seemed near akin to the silent, incomprehensible, tireless earth itself. Toward her freshness and sweetness all his being drew with a yearning like that of the tides heaving moonward from unsounded depths; though one looking on would never have guessed it.

"I'll fix you a better place to sit," he said, and his voice had the sweetness of bees droning in honey-drunken meadows. It was an odd, murmuring speech, coming and lapsing like natural sounds, but very pleasant to hear.

"I can see better from here," Georgia argued, tucking one foot under her. "What's that you're making? I want to watch you work."

"Jist a cow-bell," replied Return Ritchie. "Man up the valley's got two heifers might' near alike, and it's his notion to bell 'em as near the same as he can; so I'm aimin' to match this here." He showed his model, and sounded it so that the clear tone filled the cavern of liquid-cool shadow. They smiled at each other, and he turned to blow the forge fire. A red flare shot up and illumined the smoky walls.

With the big pincers he drew out of the coals a thin sheet of iron cut into the required shape. She watched him bend it round the anvil's beak and deftly seam the sides before the metal darkened. Afterward he riveted the seams, fixed a staple rivet in the top to hold the clapper, and added a bar through which to run the collar strap.

"Now it's ready for brazing?" she inquired, with interest.

"Now it's ready; only brass has got so high that they mostly have to be brazed with copper; and copper's copper these days, let me tell ye. You never see one made afore, Georgie?"

"I never did. You're always making things; that's why I stopped in—that and to see Aunt Lucy." She looked on while he laid the bits of copper over the outer surface, wrapped them in place with a wet rag, and packed the whole bell inside and out with clay. Then he fired the mass, pulling regularly on the bellows.

"Now, when I take it out the fire," he told her, "the copper'll be run in a thin coat clean over hit—all ready to put a clapper into and hang on the cow. This one here's been coppered—see?—and the copper's all wore and knocked off." He leaned that she might take the old bell from his hand.

"I expect it's traveled many a hundred miles through these woods, along of the cow, into wilder places than ever I've been," said the girl, holding it up. "Listen! Don't it ring sweet? — Do-re-me-faaaa! Return, can you read music?"

"Any Jack can read them songs they've been learning at the Blue Springs church," he allowed. "But without shaped notes I'm liable to git lost. I can't read the words any too well yit."

"I told poppa I was sure I could pick out tunes if he'd only buy me an organ; I'd love to have all-day singing at our house, and so would mother. But you know he calls all instruments 'inventions of idleness'." She laughed depreciatingly. "If I even had a fiddle, like yours— Could I play that, Return, you reckon?"

"You could learn. I'll learn you." If the words sounded gruff and ungracious, it was because he was taken unawares by the sudden opportunity. Here abruptly was the opening for which, all through the spring months, he had planned with such quiverings of hope and trepidation. Now the way was easy for presentation of his gift. Yet he found it necessary to make his approach obliquely, mountaineer fashion.

"D'you ever see a dulcimore?" he began, after a silence.

"One or two."

"How would one do, instead of a organ?"

"It would be music."

"I've — I've got one."

"You— What say, Return?"

"I've made ye one—a dulcimore." The new bell was imperilled while he groped into the recesses of his tool-box. Presently he held toward her a queerly shaped instrument of three strings, a little larger than a mandolin. It was whittled with innumerable patient touches out of dark-brown oak, unvarnished, the head resembling a fiddle's, but curiously carved in an attempt at ornamentation—a thing fitted only for the wild minors of native airs.

She took it and jumped to the ground; silent with surprise, she stood holding the dulcimore in both hands.

"I sent back where Aunt Lucy was raised, in the other valley, for the pattern," he said, uneasily. "They've got lots of 'em there. . . ."

"Did you make this for me, Return?"

He pulled at the bellows, and made believe not to hear.

"You did make this for me?" she asked again, slowly; and at her tone a tremor of joy went over his averted face.

"I knowed you liked music," he muttered, as though offering an apology.

Still wondering and admiring her gift, she seated herself in the main doorway, on the sill white with road dust, and began to draw the strings into the weird and plaintive harmony of which they were capable.

Without letting go of the bellows, he tossed into her lap a triangular plectrum of smoothed bone.

"You pick hit with that," said he; and, meeting the girl's eyes, was suddenly mastered by the laugh of utter delight that he had been trying to restrain.

A gray little figure appeared in the opposite doorway, which connected with his home cabin and truck-patch.

"I 'lowed I heared some music," quavered Return's only relative, the old aunt who had raised him. "Oh, hit's you, Georgie. Howdy, honey?" She came into the smithy, and the young man brought her a broken wagon-seat. She settled herself to look over a lapful of wild greens she had gathered.

"Eh, law!" she commented, when the dulcimore had been explained to her, "and that's what he's been a-whittlin' on all winter. Whar I come from the young gals used to sing to them things." She sat nodding and smiling, tapping the floor with her foot while Georgia coaxed a shadowy melody between false starts and fumbled fingerings. It was but a little time before impatience got the better of the air, and *Barney McCoy* fell away into faint monotonous chords.

"Well, I must be going," the girl said finally, rising. She cherished the little brown dulcimore in tender fingers, slipping her hands softly over its rough whittled sides as though she smoothed a child's tousled head. "Return," she said as she turned away, "if it's clear tonight, you come up to the house and bring your fiddle. We'll tune it with my dulcimore then. Maybe against that time I'll have learned how to play a little. If the moon shines, you and me and mother and the boys can all go down to the waterfall and sing there like we used to. Good-by, Aunt Lucy."

Fiddlin' mountain man, taken near Asheville, North Carolina, 1915

But the moon did not shine. That same evening a terrific storm, the tail of a hurricane beating up from the Gulf, swept over the valley. Throughout the half-hour of the storm's endurance the play of lightning was almost continuous. Between the twin hills, where it was caught and concentrated as if in the nose of the smithy's bellows, it went roaring like a battle. Day broke nearly cloudless over the wreckage that strewed the fields. Wherever a twist of the wind's erratic course had driven hardest, there was ruin. Return's chimney had crashed through his roof; and the old aunt's life had passed with the passing of the storm.

For weeks thereafter Return was a man lost in his own walls. He tried to go on as usual, but every hour of the day had its peculiar strangeness, upsetting all the habits of his life. The effort to eat in solitude a dish of his own contriving choked him. He had retained from his healthy childhood a sound, simple delight in the mere round of the day; but now, from the time of rising, when the early sunbeams shone on no little gray figure by the kitchen window, with deft hands moulding the morning's biscuit, to the sunset hour of rest on the deserted porch, nothing was as it should be.

"Poor Aunt Lucy! Jist looks like I cain't get over it," he muttered again and again. The presence of death seemed ever with him in its unsupportable majesty. "I reckon that's what sets people to thinkin' about ha'nts in houses," he reflected, forlornly. The unlighted lamp, the empty rooms, were terrible to him. The silence oppressed like a weight of dark waters. He mended the broken roof and rebuilt the chimney; then he resumed regular work in the blacksmith shop, and frequently prolonged his labors far into the night for sheer dread of the gaping doors.

In these days Georgia made the discovery that she had, while awaiting the Prince, unwittingly become bound to Return. She had a period of bewildered astonishment. How could this be her lover, this man of the stony soil?

One twilight, between mocking-bird and whippoorwill, sitting by the spring near her home, she told him, utterly trusting herself and him. In their great moment the habit of proud reserve cheapened suddenly to insignificance, and the shyness of youth fell from their hearts as the clay had shattered from around the perfected bell.

"I can't leave you, never, no more than if I was your mother," she said, with quaint frankness.

The dulcimore and the fiddle lay forgotten at their feet. But the gladness she looked for did not come at once into his face.

"I used to wonder sometimes, when we was little folks singin' by the falls, if you wouldn't come to me some day," he answered, gravely, with a deep tenderness. "I've always wanted you, but I had about give up. Have you thought, girl? . . . You must talk to your folks first."

"Whatever they say can't make any difference to me, Return," she promised. "I don't mind about the others; but mother—I'm afraid she's going to take it hard."

"I would do the very best I could for you, sister; you know that. But she'll think it's not good enough. . . . It's not good enough; but—"

Beyond the word there stood something too vague for expression, something great enough to face all opposing considerations with perfect calm. He wrinkled his big brows. "People have to put up with things sometimes," he brought out finally.

"And I couldn't see this coming," moaned Georgia's mother, as the two sat on the porch at twilight. "I could not see. I was afraid, too, for you to keep that dulcimore he made you; but music seemed to be your happiness—and your father wouldn't let you have the organ. Oh, I ought to have guarded you. But I never dreamed that such a man could have any attraction for a girl reared and taught as you have been. Why, Georgia, it can't be more than a passing fancy. Don't, don't you think of it longer than you can help, dear, and it'll go by. You can't mean to ruin your life!" And fear stood in her eyes.

To her, Return was little more than the freckled urchin with ready grin and a missing front tooth who had used to thank her for cookies. Georgia saw him transfigured by a light of dreams into something finer than he would ever appear to his fellows. He was still the barefoot playmate, but he was also in some way the Sungod. Which were the truer estimate, let him say who has dwelt longest in that unearthly radiance. Into the mother's mind flashed two conflicting urgencies—the need for prompt action if she would save her daughter, and the fear that one ill-considered word might fumble her slipping hold. Already she felt her grasp loosening, moment by moment, as Georgia before her eyes became a woman.

Her little girl!

Afraid to leave the subject where it had fallen, she hurried on: "Georgia, dear, you shall go down into the Valley—to the Academy—and have some music lessons. You've always wanted to; now you shall, honey; I'll manage it somehow. And time you come home I'll make your father buy you an organ, I can. I've never asked much of him; but I can make him do that."

"Music lessons—an organ!" echoed Georgia, piteously. "Why, that couldn't make any difference, mother—though I'd love to have them, to play for—him."

Her face expressed only wonder and pity. Poor mother! Did she believe the whole world of music would count for a minute against Return? There was no hesitation, no complexity, in the girl's mental processes. She had given herself to love—to her lover—she was wondering now how best to comfort her mother. It was as simple as a plant's attitude toward the sun.

The mother, leaning forward, clutched the slim wrists of the girl with both her dingy, toil-maimed hands. In her extremity she sought for help whence help had never come to her.

"Has he asked your father for you, then?" she inquired, huskily. "And you never spoke one word to me about it! Georgia, my poor child, this is worse than ever I thought. Oh, put it out of your mind. If you are too young to realize what is due to yourself, try to think, dear, is nothing due to me, your mother? I was nursing you and slaving for you when Return Ritchie was riding stick horses!"

"Yes, he asked father," the girl said, gently. "He says poppa told him I could do as I pleased. Poppa likes him." A little wistfully: "I'm sorry Return spoke to him before I named it to you."

"You're blinded," spoke Selina, heavily. "You can't see now; but when you wake up and find yourself dragged down to the level of his people, it will break your heart."

Looking into the young face, its roseate velvet all atremble with new emotions, the mother felt as though striving in a nightmare with bending, splintering weapons. She had reason to know that she was impotently dashing herself upon no human adversary, but one of those laws that seemed always arrayed against her, always defeating her heart's hopes, always crushing her pitilessly. Had she not fought this same losing fight once before? She had never forgotten the days and weeks before her own marriage; the struggling, resisting, calling to her aid all habit and tradition, all maidenly reserve and family pride—in vain. She had suffered in withstanding; she had suffered in yielding; and her suffering had not mattered in the least, would not matter now. Oh, the big blind forces, the dark brute powers! Why was it allowed, this stupendous cruelty? Who allowed it? She was near to arraigning the great laws of the universe.

Yet she gathered herself for the battle. Before, it had been to save herself from she knew not what; now, with experience behind her, she would fight to save her daughter from a fate all too bitterly certain. She would appeal to Return also, to the rude and genuine good heart of him. There, if nowhere else, might be a chance. . . .

"Oh, listen to reason, Georgia, before it's too late. You don't know—" Her tongue ran into wild and futile repetitions. She became conscious of them and caught herself up. "Dear, you can't see what is ahead of you, or you would not think for a moment of doing this thing. Only let me tell you what it has been like with me. I never would let you know—I hoped I should never have to tell you. Just listen to me . . ."

She poured it all forth now, the story of the bitter years. . . . "And they don't care," she whispered. "They don't know. Nobody knows but your own self. You never saw your uncles. My brothers wouldn't visit us. When things were at their worst they wrote and wrote, urging me to come back, to leave him; offering a home, offering work, offering to educate the children—anything, if I only would. Seemed like they couldn't give me up to lead such a life. They don't write any more now, of course—but then . . . One baby after another. Yet the babies were all that kept me alive. It's a miracle any of you got through; we hadn't any decent—arrangements. Oh, I suppose I was all that kept them alive, too—my body held between you-all and death. You look as though you thought that was something glorious! I tell you there's nothing romantic about cooking three meals a day with a teething baby on one arm and your face tied up with neuralgia. Nothing heroic about washing overalls, or following your man to the barn with a lantern at two o'clock on a February night to tend to young lambs, either. And look at me!" She stood up, a scarred and darkened ruin. "Look at me! It's what you'll be; it's the best you can hope to be. You that I slaved for—you that I nursed—the only one that is mine! Georgia, daughter, tell me you won't do it!"

"I won't, mother!" cried the girl, the heart wrung out of her by grief and compassion. "I'll stay with you. Return will understand. I'll take care of you—"

"No! I won't have you sacrifice your life for me any more than for him. Oh, you don't know. . . . It would be easy enough to die for a man; it's hard to live for him—to give him all your life just when you want it most yourself. And when you think you have given the last that is in you,

17

comes a new demand. You can't back out; you've got to meet it. Why, I've done things I can't talk about even now—things any woman will tell you she can't do. I had to! Take care of me? Why, I'm easy now; I've reached the best life holds for me so far as rest and plenty are concerned. The hard work is over, and the long pain, and the cold, and the worry. But the disappointment will never be over."

She was striving for self-control now, overcoming by main strength an impulse toward the hysteric crying of despair.

"And it's no use! I see by your face that it's no use talking. Was it for this I have stood between you and the work and the hardships—have I carried the burden for years on my own shoulders only to see you take it up at last? Oh, I've waited and watched, praying for a chance to send you away—to lift you out of such a life. I want you to have a chance...."

Poor woman! she had meant to be all in all to her child, at least until the coming of larger opportunity. And now here lay her treasure on the quicksands!

"But — Love?" whispered the girl, blushing exquisitely. "It was you, mother, taught me what love means. I—I used to wonder how you could bear—poppa's ways, until I came to see that you accepted them as parts of him, like his voice and hair; and you accepted him twenty years ago. People think their children don't notice; but— it's beautiful, beautiful, mother."

There was a wonderful light in the eyes she raised timidly, pleadingly, to the elder woman in the soft dusk.

"I taught you?" Selina's voice was hard. "Well, then, I can teach you the better, maybe, that this feeling you have now — won't last. It can't last. You believe it will, but it can't. Do you suppose I didn't have it? Ah! you think it lasted — for me?" She laughed bitterly. "Georgia, if you throw yourself away, I have lost all that made

A mountain fireside, taken near Asheville, North Carolina, 1915

life bearable." Her face fell into lines of gloomy reverie as she looked away.

"She is remembering," thought the girl. "She had love once; she was young; she hardly knew what trouble was, or pain. Now there is only heartache." She called up in her own memory as much as she had known or guessed of her mother's trials, and her eyes filled with tears. Yet it detracted nothing from the mysterious splendor of her own fate that its terror must be set over against its beauty. The glamour which invested her lover's figure would be no less bright if her crown promised to be one of thorns.

"Love," the woman's voice touched the word as though it were something hot which burned. The eyes of her spirit seemed to glance at it as though its brightness seared. "Love— Oh, Georgia, you don't know." Her tones sank, her head drooped forward; but she spoke again. "When I first came here, to teach the little school in the cove, I was as full of dreams as you are. I had money saved to finish my education; I wanted to be somebody. But I waked up and found myself married . . ."

The girl cried: "But you don't have to live so! What makes you?" Swift indignation at the man who had claimed all this possessed her. Less wise than her mother, she did not see past him to the eternal law, the Way of Things, of which he was but an expression.

"What makes me?" A dull interrogation showed through the blank and beaten face.

"Why don't you go to your people?" pursued Georgia. "Why haven't you gone long ago? Back to your own life!"

Selina stared for a second, and then threw out both hands with a motion as of casting something from her.

"Oh, I couldn't do that," she wailed. "Georgia, what would become of him?"

The girl's eyes, already wonder-filled, widened and widened as the full significance of these words went home.

"You see!" she breathed.

"See what?" queried the elder, tonelessly, detecting a low note of something akin to triumph in the cry.

"Mother!" She clasped her warm young arms round the bent and quaking shoulders. "Mother! Don't you see, now—" The rest was a whisper. "Now you *have* showed me—what love is, what it means to us women."

Selina sobbed on uncomforted for a time. At last she became quiet, and leaning her head on her hands, sighed wearily.

Dusk had deepened almost to night about them, sparkling with fireflies and throbbing to wilder songs than are heard by day. From the turn of the lane, where all the sweetness of the blossoming earth was being evoked by the dew, came suddenly the cooing of strings beneath a bow's caress. The girl's eyes lighted softly.

"I don't know," said Selina, without raising her head. "He's not fit for you. But . . . he will always be a good man. And"—nervelessly—"it's the only way to live, I suppose. Maybe—by and by—I can be reconciled. But—My poor daughter!"

The strings sounded again, nearer, and as though at the touch of the unseen wapentake the girl rose. She looked long down the shadowy vista with that light upon her face that can shine but once in a lifetime; then turning, she reached from its shelf within the house door the little dulcimore that held all of music her life would ever attain.

Origins of the Appalachian Dulcimer

Many theories have originated concerning the Appalachian dulcimer's origins, though none of them have been substantiated as yet. In fact, it was only quite recently that the history of this obscure mountain instrument has even whetted the curiosity of scholars. Most early folk music research centered around song lyric origins, not instrument origins.

There are several reasons why the Appalachian dulcimer's ancestry is difficult to trace with precision. Currently, there are no old living dulcimer makers or players. Also, the dulcimer belongs to a class of instruments called the fretted zithers which have existed in many cultures. In addition to this, there was another instrument in common usage early in the United States called the English hammered dulcimer which was usually referred to in literature as a dulcimer. The English hammered dulcimer dates back thousands of years to ancient Greece. This instrument, mentioned in the Bible frequently, is often confused with the Appalachian dulcimer. Although the English hammered dulcimer and the Appalachian dulcimer are historically unrelated, it appears likely that the Appalachian dulcimer was named after the English hammered dulcimer for two reasons.

Firstly, both the hammered and the Appalachian dulcimer possess a similar sweet song which is what dulcimer means translated from the Greek "dulce," or sweet, and the Latin "melos," or song. Also, England was the sole northern European country without an instrument related to the dulcimer. This meant that most English immigrants had never seen an instrument resembling an Appalachian dulcimer before arriving in the United States. From a British perspective, then, dulcimer was the most logical name for this instrument, since its tone so closely resembled their own hammered dulcimer. The name endured, since the British formed the bulk of the Appalachian settlers.

Although the Appalachian dulcimer received its name from the English hammered dulcimer, the instrument itself is thought to be related to several European instruments, all of which greatly resemble the Appalachian dulcimer in their playing style, shape, and string arrangement. All of the Appalachian dulcimer's European predecessors were relegated to the status of folk instruments during the Renaissance, since they were not as versatile as the new instruments being created at that time.

The dulcimer's first traceable European ancestor is the German scheitholt, whose first written description appeared in 1618 in the book *Syntagama Musicum* by Praetorius. The scheitholt probably originated in the Middle Ages due to its close relationship to a group of medieval instruments and its early distribution to all parts of Europe.

Praetorius described the scheitholt as a small monochord provided at one end with a peg box possessing three or four strings all tuned to the same note except for the last string which was tuned an octave higher. Normally its body possessed straight sides, and the frets were placed on the sounding board which also served as a fret board. The instrument was strummed with the thumb crossing all of the strings, while a small rod served to fret the melody string. Many instruments closely resembling the scheitholt have been found in the Appalachians, the result of the Southern Highlands receiving a large influx of German settlers. After the scheitholt became established in Germany, it gradually found its way to neighboring countries where it was redesigned to conform to the local musical cultures. This makes it quite difficult to follow the scheitholt's early European development.

The Vosges Mountains of France was one of the first places the scheitholt was found outside of Germany. The scheitholt was first believed to be Flemish by the French. Later it was nationalized, however, and named the Epinette des Vosges, after an evergreen tree that grows in the Vosges Mountains. During the next several hundred years the Epinette des Vosges was modified very little. It retained its oblong body which supported five strings. Two of these were fretted with a smooth rod, while a goose quill picked all of the strings. The strings were tuned to the exact pitch as a dulcimer in the traditional major tuning: G, G, C.

Some time after the scheitholt arrived in France, it traveled to Scandinavia. It first appeared in Sweden and was named the humle.

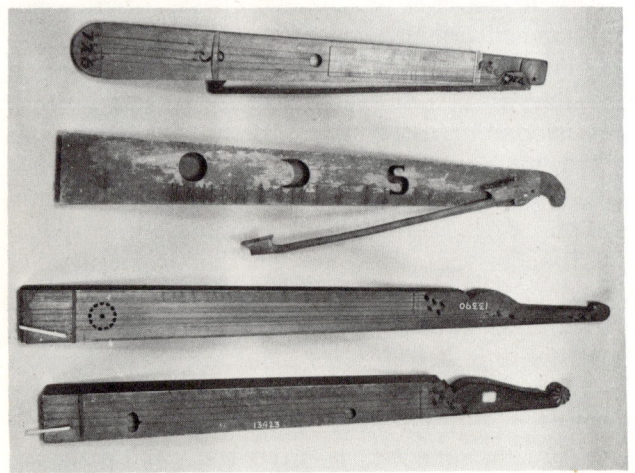

German scheitholts, bowed and plucked, retrieved in the Appalachians

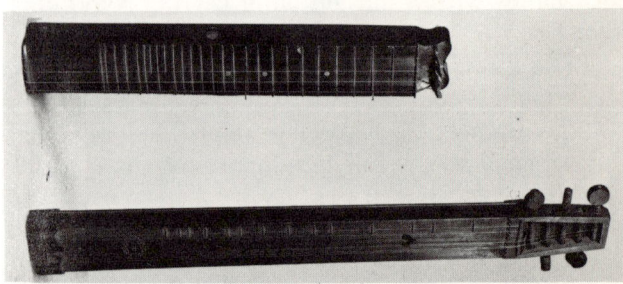

German scheitholts, made in the 18th century

French Epinette des Vosges, made in the mid 19th century

Otto Malmberg playing his humle, 1917

Otto Malmberg and his Swedish humle, 1917

There it took on various shapes. The sound box often exhibited a characteristic bulge on one or both sides, although a bulge on one side was more common. The Swedes added iron tuning pins, a distinctive fret board, and an elaborate scroll to the humle. These refinements made the humle a more advanced instrument than the scheitholt, its predecessor. Occasionally an old humle is found in Sweden that differs little from the scheitholt. Otto Malmberg, the last known Swedish humle player, who died in 1921, is pictured here. The humle that he is shown playing was handed down from his great grandfather, who also passed on the technique of playing it using musical thirds. This was accomplished by fretting the double melody strings two frets apart, while all of the strings were strummed in the same direction with a plectrum made from a slate pencil.

Swedish humles

Norwegian langeleik player

Later the humle appeared in Norway where it was called the langeleik. It was first mentioned in Norwegian literature by Anders Arrebo in the early seventeenth century, when he referred to it as a langspil. The langeleik's shape was refined by the Norwegians to a long hollow box with seven or eight strings. These strings were adjusted with wooden pegs which were secured in a violin type peg box. Some old langeleiks even had a peg box at both ends of the fret board. Occasionally fine tuners were present for subtle tone adjustments. These tuners consisted of small sliding wooden blocks near the ends of the strings opposite the main tuning mechanisms. A langeleik's strings were struck with a long elastic horn, while the three middle fingers of the left hand fretted the strings. This made it possible to sound complicated embellishments which are very characteristic of Norwegian folk music. Up to the eighteenth century the langeleik was the most beloved instrument of the Norwegian peasants, but by the nineteenth century it had almost vanished from use. Recently a folk revival occurred in Norway, and now langeleik competitions are held frequently. This instrument probably had a great influence on the dulcimer's development, since many langeleiks were brought to the Appalachians by Norwegian immigrants. In fact, a number of langeleiks have been housed in American museums since the early eighteenth century.

From Norway the langeleik traveled to Iceland where it was transformed to an instrument named the langspil. The langspil's first literary appearance occurred when it was listed in Jon Olafson's dictionary in the early 1800's. The langspil was shaped as a long box rounded off at one end with a large sound hole in this bulge. It also had violin type tuning pegs which held two strings tuned in unison, and a third string tuned an octave lower. Although the fingers originally strummed the strings, it later became acceptable to bow the langspil's strings. The rise in the popularity of the bowing technique probably resulted from another Icelandic instrument called the filda which was played with a bow. Today the langspil is almost nonexistent in Iceland.

After evolving in Scandinavia for several hundred years, the scheitholt was transported to Holland in a rather modified form and named the humle or hommel. While in most countries the scheitholt had been named after its physical appearance, in Holland it was named after the tone that it produced. Hommel or humle is a derivation of the Dutch verb hommeln which means to hum, an apt description of the drone strings tone. In Holland the humle took on various shapes, although it usually had iron tuning pins and approximately ten strings on a raised finger board which were either strummed, bowed, or plucked. The wide variety of picking techniques employed on the humle in Holland was the result of the instrument being carried there by sailors from various northern European countries where the scheitholt had developed differently.

The scheitholt, then, had a rather long life in Europe. It originated in Germany in the Middle Ages, made its way early in its life to France, then to Scandinavia, and returned to southern Europe in a modified form. Wherever it traveled, the scheitholt was adapted to the existing musical culture.

In the early 1920's, Josiah H. Combs believed that the dulcimer was an attempt to recreate the German scheitholt. Combs suggested that the

Icelandic langspil player, 1890

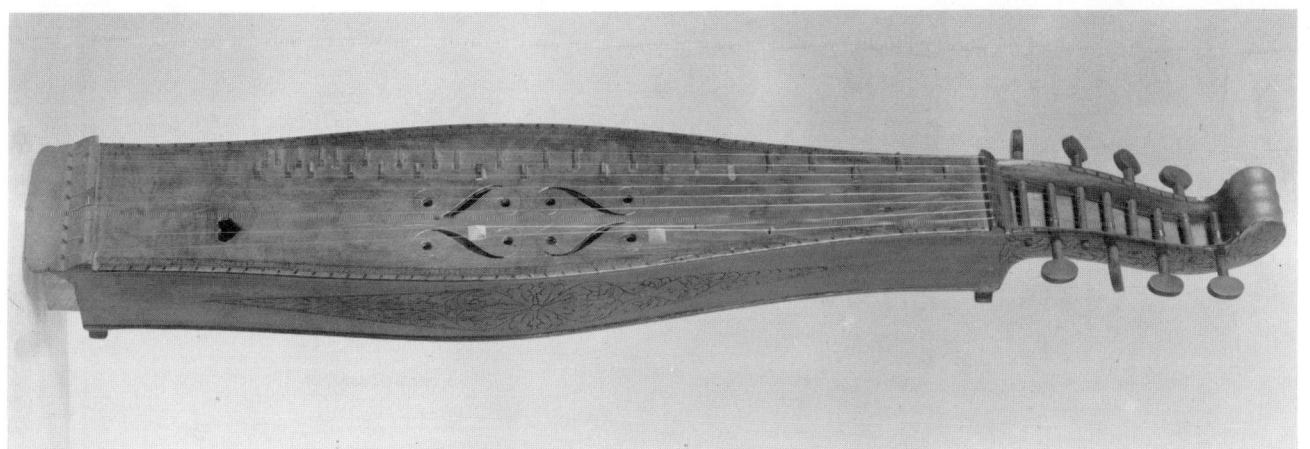

Norwegian langeleik, made in the 18th century

Jethro Ambergy, woodworking teacher, Hindman, Kentucky, circa 1929

scheitholt took on various shapes in the mountains resulting from the few crude tools that were available there. However, since then many instruments have been retrieved in the Appalachians resembling European instruments related to the scheitholt. The dulcimer does not duplicate any of these instruments. It seems more likely that the dulcimer was an outgrowth of a variety of European instruments, created from the memory of the German, Norwegian, Dutch, and Swedish immigrants who settled in the Appalachians.

The development of the Appalachian dulcimer probably parallels the development of the Highlander's music, both of which were shaped by many diverse cultures converging in the mountains where frills were expendable.

Early Dulcimer Construction

One reason why the dulcimer developed in the Southern Highlands was its ease of construction. Until recently, the building techniques for this instrument had been transferred within the bounds of oral tradition. This accounts for the wide variety of shapes and materials used in dulcimer construction. Dulcimers were generally built according to the following methods, although the specifics were determined to a great extent by a maker's experience, taste, and access to tools and materials.

From the virgin forests, wood from trees such as walnut, cherry, and poplar could be easily obtained for building a dulcimer. The logs from these trees were cut open with a crosscut saw or by a sawmill if there was one in the area. This provided rough planks that were thinned to the proper thickness with a hand plane or a drawknife, accounting for the roughly finished wood in early instruments. After the wood had been hewn to its final dimensions, the sides were bent with steam and then placed in a mold to set. The top, back, and sides were then glued together in a shape resembling a teardrop or an hourglass with hide glue which was obtained from melting down the hoofs and cartilage of animals. The head and the fret board were then glued to the body of the instrument, while tapered wooden dowels strengthened these glue joints.

The specific features of different dulcimers varied greatly. Most had between two and eight strings of gut or anvil hammered iron wire, although three or four strings was the most prevalent. A violin type scroll was common on dulcimers, although much less elaborate in design. The scroll is the end of the instrument's head. The sounding boards had either two or four sound holes in the shape of diamonds, hearts, circles, or f-holes, the same design used on violins. Wooden tuning pegs, almost identical to a violin's, were most commonly used. Hand forged metal pins, squared off at one end so that they could be adjusted with a clock winding mechanism, also served as tuning pegs. Early dulcimers were frequently painted instead of being finished with clear lacquer or oil as instruments are today.

The fret arrangements and the fret materials varied greatly. Some instruments had frets under the first string only, others had frets under all of the strings, while others had a combination of short and long frets. Frets were most commonly fashioned of easily accessible broom maker's wire, although iron or brass wire was sometimes used. To form a fret, wire was bent in the shape of a staple and then driven into the finger board. Occasionally bone or ivory was carved into frets and glued on the finger board.

Three design variations were used to increase a dulcimer's resonance. The first variation consisted of small wooden knobs placed on the bottom of the sounding box. If the dulcimer was played on a table, these knobs enabled the entire table top to act as a secondary sounding board. Another more elaborate feature included in some dulcimers was a sounding post, a small piece of wood which was wedged in the instrument between the sounding board and the back of the body. A sounding post transfers the vibrations from the sounding board to the instrument's back, enabling the back to resonate equally as well as the sounding board. The last design variation included notching or hollowing out the fret board which permitted the sounding board to resonate more freely.

In addition to dulcimers with one fret board, there was another more uncommon style dulcimer with a dual fret board and a peg box at one end of each fret board. This instrument was dubbed a harmonium or sometimes a courtin dulcimer, since it enabled lovers to rub knees as they played duets and gazed into one another's eyes.

Made by J. E. Thomas, Bath, Kentucky, 1927

Made by W. Ham, North Carolina, mid 19th century

Made by Charles Hammack, Clendenin, West Virginia, 1850

Made by George Daugherty, Grinder, Kentucky, 19th century

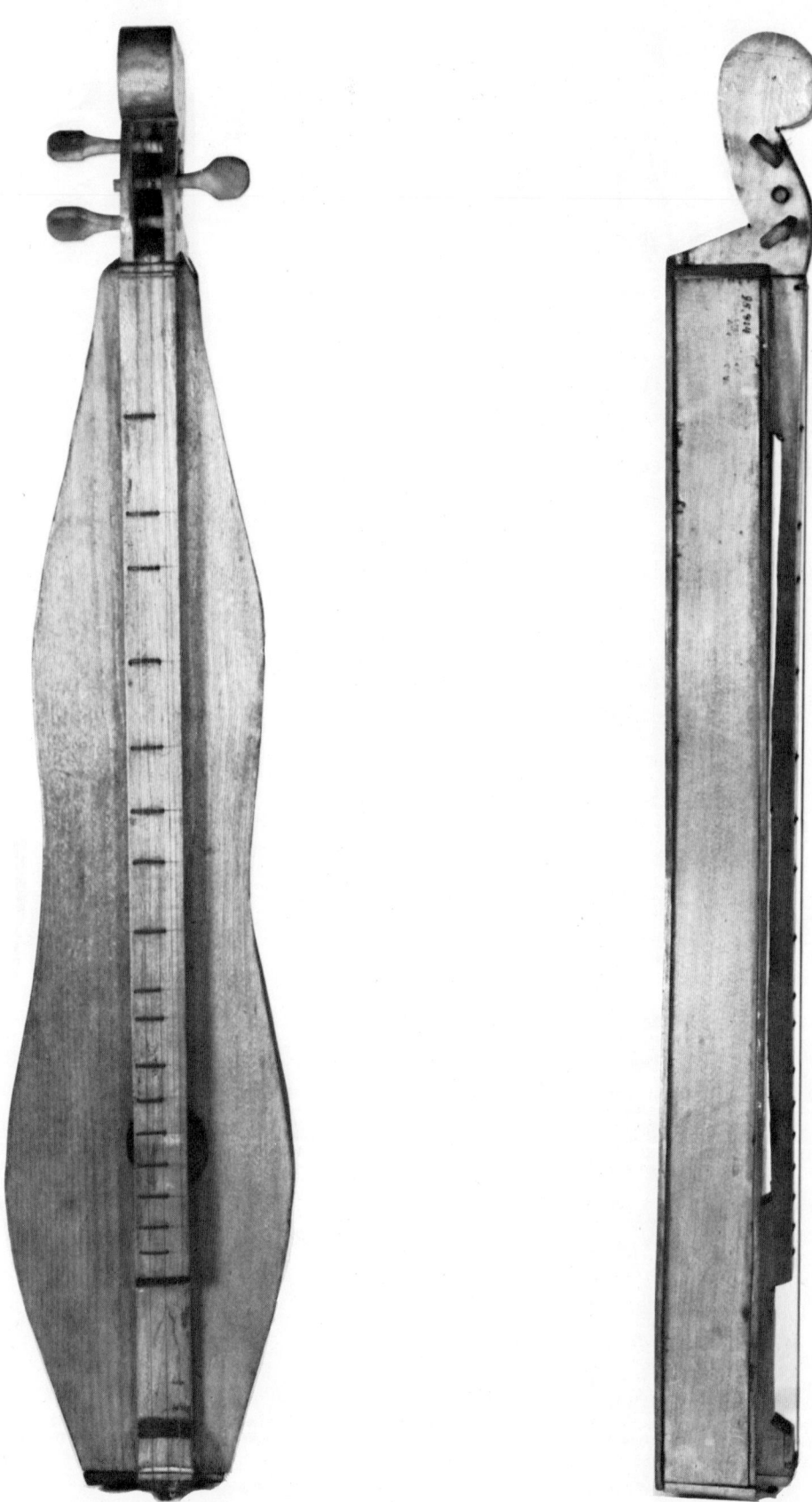

Made by P. L. Clayton, Allegheny County, Virginia, 1895

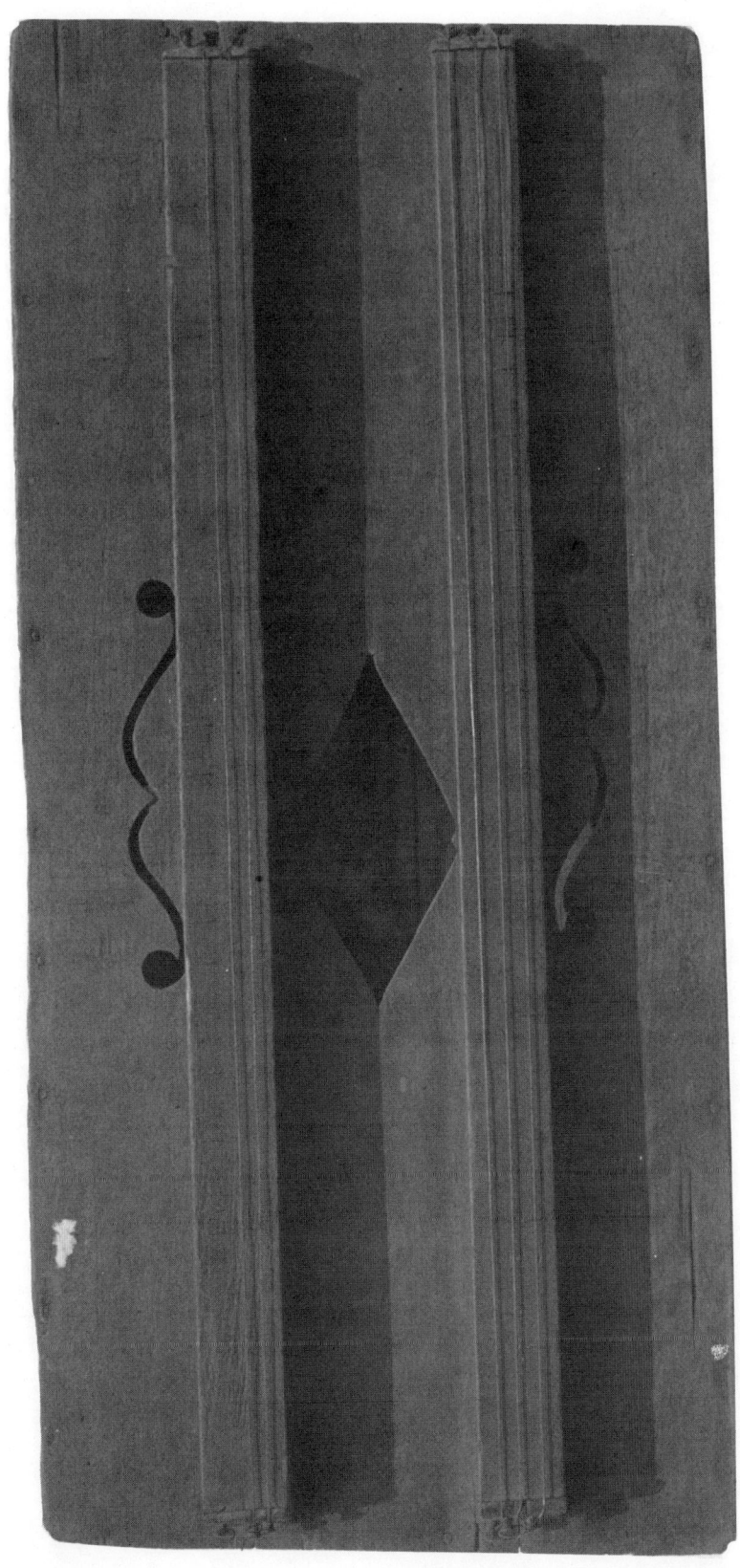

Courtin dulcimer, given to Levi Jackson State Park Museum, Kentucky, 1944, by William Price, Corbin, Kentucky. Had belonged to Rev. Harvey Burnett of Somerset, Kentucky.

Early Dulcimer Makers

Many dulcimer makers devoted their entire lives to the tradition of dulcimer making. Several of these craftsmen's lives were documented. The following excerpt, which originally appeared in Allen Eaton's *Handicrafts of the Southern Highlands*, gives a brief account of the life of Edward Thomas, one of the earliest known Appalachian dulcimer makers.

•Mr. Thomas, the most outstanding dulcimer maker of the Highlands, was born about 1850 in Letcher County, Kentucky. He began making dulcimers when he was twenty-one years old, continuing with considerable regularity until shortly before his death in 1933, a working period of nearly sixty-two years. He is said to have numbered the instruments. It is believed by some of his acquaintances that he may have made as many as 1,500 all told. There is no record showing exactly what disposition was made of all of these, but probably Mr. Thomas' statement that "they went to all lands everywhere" is not too vague if we think of all lands as meaning the United States and England. Most of them, he is reported to have said, were sold in New York because there were "more people there than anywhere else." He sold a considerable number by mail, and these sometimes gave him trouble. His nephew at one time said that "Uncle Eddie" had made a dulcimer for the Prince of Wales, but he had not sent it yet because he did not know his post-office address. The instrument finally went, however, and Mr. Thomas related the agreeable news that "the king" had written him a nice letter "with a lot of gold and purple in it," but one of the children he said burned the letter by mistake, "so he couldn't show it to anyone any more!"

°Mr. Thomas made his dulcimers usually of walnut though sometimes of maple or birch, and a few of California redwood which he said came from "far over the seas." His earlier ones were carefully put together, but time and weather have loosened some of the joints and in his late years the craftsmanship did not come up to that in the early ones. His favorite design for the holes in the body of the dulcimer was heart shaped. The decoration around the heart is painted in gold on a few of his instruments.

•Allen Eaton, *Handicrafts of the Southern Highlands*, Russell Sage Foundation, New York, 1937, pages 202, 203.

° Photographs of one of Edward Thomas's dulcimers can be found on page 26.

Unidentified dulcimer maker (along with examples of his work in the construction stage, circa 1930)

MAKING MUSIC

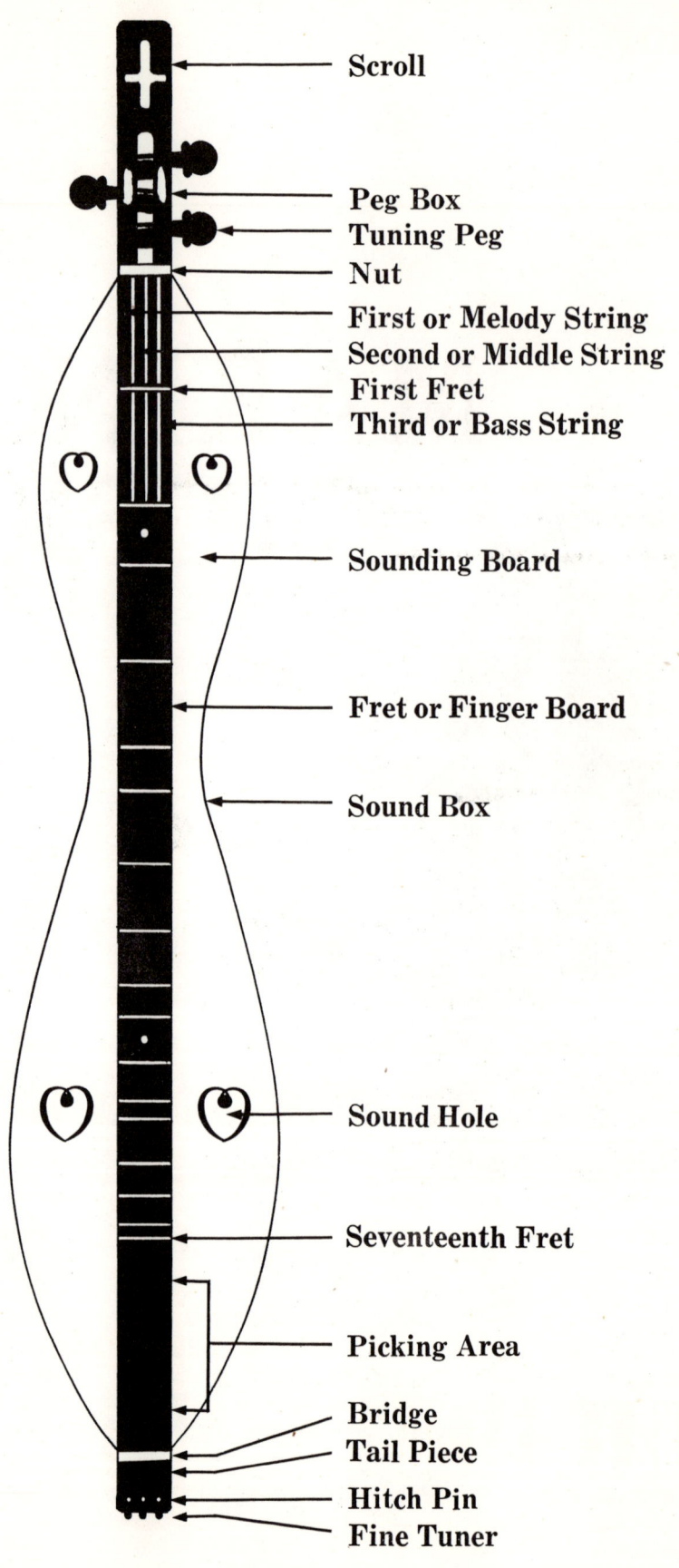

Introduction to Playing

Some old mountain folks declared, "You can't play a proper tune on a dulcimer without a gander quill for the pick and a goose quill for the noter." Others believed each instrument had a secret pitch known only by the owner where it sounded best. As you can see, the dulcimer is a very personal instrument with no set playing styles. However, the remainder of this chapter will attempt to set down some musical basics to help you begin playing. In order to avoid confusion, you should be familiar with the names of the parts of the dulcimer listed in the diagram.

Modal Music

Modal music is the musical system on which the dulcimer is based. Although it is not absolutely essential to understand modal music to play the dulcimer, it will help to explain why the strings are tuned to certain pitches, why the frets are arranged in a peculiar order, and give you an understanding about how to tune a dulcimer to another instrument.

The dulcimer, like any other instrument, is characterized by its own limitations which lend to it a discernible quality. One distinguishing characteristic of the dulcimer is its fret arrangement. When the melody string, the string on which a dulcimer's scale is located, is fretted, the notes have the same tonal relationships as the white keys on a piano. This is because the fretted melody string on a dulcimer and the white keys on a piano represent notes that can be divided up into scales containing seven notes, A to G. The notes that make up these scales repeat themselves the entire length of the fret board on the dulcimer and the keyboard on the piano.

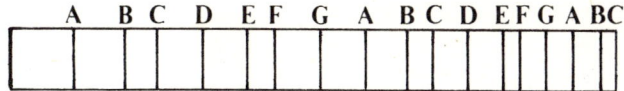

A dulcimer's sporadic fret arrangement is most easily understood by comparing it with a piano's keyboard. On a piano each key, black or white, represents a musical half tone. However, there are no black keys between the white keys B and C, and E and F. This means that these white keys are separated by only half a tone, while all of the other white keys are separated by a full tone.

Intervals Between All Keys

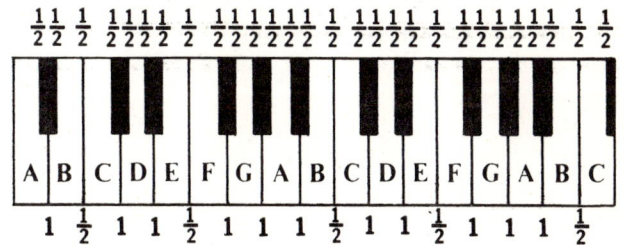

Intervals Between White Keys

Since the fretted melody string on the dulcimer has the same tonal intervals as the white keys on a piano, the frets that represent the notes B and C, and E and F, are spaced closer together than the frets representing the remainder of the notes separated by a full tone.

Letter Name Of Fret

Intervals Between Frets

As you can see, a piano's white key scale or a dulcimer's fretted melody string scale is comprised of five full tones and two half tones. The general name for any scale possessing these intervals is a diatonic scale. Diatonic scales are what modal music is based on, whereas chromatic music is characterized by both black and white piano keys.

It is possible to play several different modal scales on the dulcimer's melody string, each of which sounds quite distinct. This is because the intervals between the notes, the whole and half tones, occur in different progressions in each mode, the result of each mode beginning on its own distinctive note or fret. For instance, if a modal scale begins on a C, the third fret, the intervals between the notes in this mode would be:

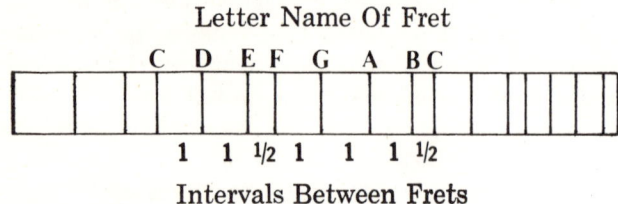

Intervals Between Frets

However, if a modal scale begins on a G, the seventh fret, the intervals between the notes in this mode would be:

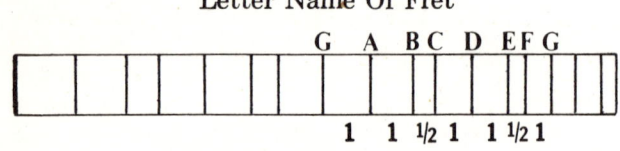

Intervals Between Frets

Since each mode begins on a particular note or fret which determines the intervals between the notes in that modal scale; and since the notes in a scale repeat themselves every seven notes, there are only seven possible modal scales:

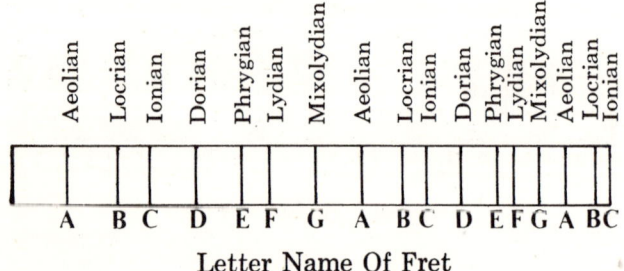

Letter Name Of Fret

Each mode can be tuned to one key at a time. The key of a mode is determined by the name of the note on which the modal scale begins, the keynote. Each modal scale was traditionally characterized by one particular key. However, the key of a modal scale can be changed or transposed to any key. To change the key of a mode, raise or lower all of the strings equally in pitch from the traditional tuning for the mode. This alters only the keynote or first note of the mode. The mode still begins on the same fret, and the intervals between the notes in the mode remain unchanged.

For instance, assume a dulcimer is tuned to the Ionian mode in the key of C, the key of the traditional Ionian mode. The strings are tuned to G, G, C. The scale begins on C, the third fret on the first string. Suppose the pitch of all the strings was raised one tone to A, A, D. This would mean that the dulcimer was transposed from the key of C to the key of D in the Ionian tuning, since the scale would now begin on a D, the third fret on the first string.

Once again, the key to which the dulcimer is tuned is determined by the keynote, the pitch of the note on which the modal scale begins. The mode to which the dulcimer is tuned is determined by the intervals between the notes in the scale, which is determined by the fret on which the modal scale begins. A dulcimer can be tuned to only one mode and to one key in that mode at a time, and it must be retuned to be played in a different mode or key.

Tuning

At first some problems may be encountered in tuning your dulcimer, particularly if you have never tuned an instrument before. However, with a little practice your ear will acquire the needed sensitivity.

You must have the proper strings on your dulcimer before it can be tuned. The strings used on five string banjos are the most versatile for a wide range of playing. Banjo second or thirteen gauge strings can be used for the melody and middle strings. A wound banjo fourth or twenty gauge string can be used for the bass string. Strings are sometimes sold by gauges only. The string gauges can be varied to permit the instrument to be tuned to a higher or lower key. However, the suggested gauges will enable you to play most songs without the strings breaking or rattling on the frets. Banjo strings come with two types of ends, "loop" and "ball." You should know what type of end will work on your dulcimer before you buy your strings.

To place a string on a dulcimer, the loop or ball end is fastened to the hitching post, while the other end of the string is wrapped around the tuning peg about three times. If a string revolves around a peg more than this, the string may become tangled, particularly if the peg is wooden. Preferably the strings should be wound under the pegs. This allows the tuning pressure to be applied toward your lap, so that the dulcimer doesn't slide. If your dulcimer has wooden pegs, tuning pressure should be applied inward gradually to fasten the pegs securely.

Two methods can be used to tune a dulcimer. The first method consists of tuning the dulcimer to itself. This allows you to tune your dulcimer where it and your voice sound the best. To tune the instrument to itself, the bass string is adjusted to where it sounds pleasing. That is, not so loose that it vibrates on the frets, but not so tight that it might break. The other strings are then tuned from the bass string using the tuning chart which outlines tuning the strings to different modes.

For instance, to tune the dulcimer to itself in the Ionian mode, adjust the bass string as just described, then depress it just to the left of the fourth fret and tune the remaining open strings to the fretted bass string. Tuning the dulcimer to itself will normally mean that you are playing in a key other than the traditional key which characterized each mode, since no effort has been made to tune the strings to a particular key.

However, if you wish to accompany another instrument, you will have to tune your dulcimer to a particular key. To do this, adjust the open bass string to the note named by the key in which you wish to play. Then tune the remainder of the strings from the bass string to place the instrument in the proper mode.

For instance, if you wish to tune the dulcimer to the traditional Ionian mode characterized by the key of C, tune the open bass string to a C using another reference instrument. Then tune the remainder of the strings from the bass string to put the dulcimer in the Ionian mode. That is, depress the bass string to the left of the fourth fret and tune the remaining open strings to the fretted bass string. This method can be used to tune the instrument to any key in any mode.

Aside from the major Ionian mode which contains no sharps or flats, there are six other modes to which the dulcimer can be tuned. All of these other modes contain sharps or flats at various intervals on their scales and are useful for playing songs which don't sound best played in the major mode. To select the proper mode for a song, you must determine the scale that it uses. For instance, if a song uses a scale with a flatted seventh, the Mixolydian mode is required; however, if a song uses a scale with a flatted third and flatted seventh, the Dorian mode is required. To find out where the sharps or flats occur in the scales of other modes, refer to the tuning chart.

A convenient tuning position

MODE	*TUNING INSTRUCTIONS	MODE BEGINS ON
Aeolian	Sound the bass string on the sixth fret and tune the first string to this note. Then sound the bass string on the fourth fret and tune the middle string to this note.	First or Eighth Fret
Locrian	Not used in folk music.	Second or Ninth Fret
Ionian	Sound the bass string on the fourth fret and tune all of the other strings to this note.	Third Fret
Dorian	Sound the bass string on the third fret and tune the first string to this note. Then sound the bass string on the fourth fret and tune the middle string to this note.	Fourth Fret
Phrygian	Sound the bass string on the fourth fret and tune the middle string to this note. Then sound the open middle string and tune the first string fretted on the second fret to the open middle string.	Fifth Fret
Lydian	Sound the bass string on the first fret and tune the first string to this note. Then sound the bass string on the fourth fret and tune the middle string to this note.	Sixth Fret
Mixolydian	Sound the bass string on the seventh fret and tune the first string to this note. Then sound the bass string on the fourth fret and tune the middle string to this note.	Open or Seventh Fret

*On a four string dulcimer, the second string is tuned to the same pitch as the melody string and is fretted simultaneously with the melody string.

TRADITIONAL KEYNOTE	INTERVALS BETWEEN NOTES	MODE SUNG AS
A	1-½-1-1-½-1-1	do re mi-flat fa sol la-flat ti-flat do
B	½-1-1-½-1-1-1	do re-flat mi-flat fa sol-flat la-flat ti-flat do
C	1-1-½-1-1-1-½	do re mi fa sol la ti do
D	1-½-1-1-1-½-1	do re mi-flat fa sol la ti-flat do
E	½-1-1-1-½-1-1	do re-flat mi-flat fa sol la-flat ti-flat do
F	1-1-1-½-1-1-½	do re mi fa-sharp sol la ti do
G	1-1-½-1-1-½-1	do re mi fa sol la ti-flat do

Unidentified dulcimer player with his wife, circa 1930

All of the modal scales used on the dulcimer are very old. In fact, they are said to be named after the Greek tribes that invented them. Chromatic music commonly used today was derived from modal scales. The Ionian mode was the basis of major music and the Aeolian mode was the basis of minor music.

About half of the songs sung in the Appalachians were in the Ionian mode. The other half of the songs were fairly evenly divided between the Mixolydian, Aeolian, and Dorian modes.

Reading Music

Two types of musical notation are used in this book. Standard musical notation represents the song's melody as it is sung. Tablature, an ancient form of musical notation prevalent up to the Middle Ages, represents the dulcimer music. If you have little prior musical knowledge, a few essentials are presented here.

Standard musical notation consists of notes on a staff. The location of a note on a staff determines the note's pitch, while the note itself signifies its relative time value. Standard musical notation is represented by four types of notes:

eighth notes: ♪ half notes: 𝅗𝅥

quarter notes: ♩ whole notes: 𝅝

Relative Time Value Of Notes

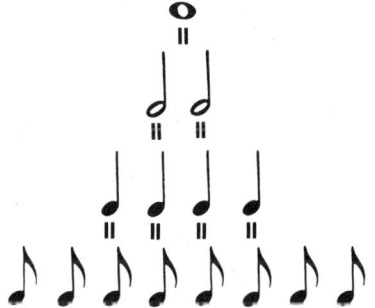

To find the exact time value each of these notes gets in a song, you must look at the song's time signature, the two numbers that appear one on top of the other at the beginning of each musical staff.

The bottom number of the time signature tells you what type of note gets one beat. For instance, if there is a four at the bottom of the time signature, it means that a quarter note gets one beat.

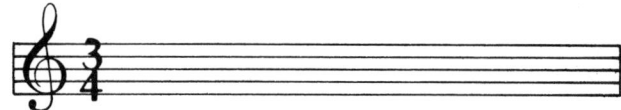

If there is an eight at the bottom of the time signature, it means that an eighth note gets one beat.

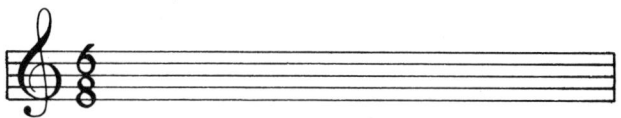

The top number of the time signature tells you how many beats there are in one measure. Measures are groups of notes, divided by vertical lines on the staff, which contain an equal number of beats.

If there is a four on top of the time signature, this means there are four beats in one measure.

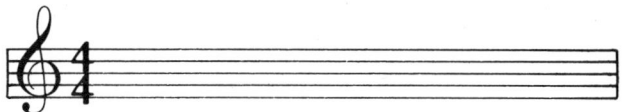

If there is a three on top of the time signature, this means that there are only three beats in one measure.

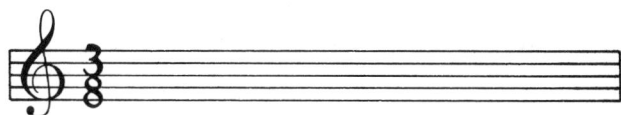

Counting the beats in the following measures with their respective time signatures is done as follows:

However, counting the beats in measures is not always this simple. Sometimes two notes are included in one beat. Since the time value of each of these notes must be counted, the two notes are counted as "one and." In the measure below two eighth notes are included in one beat. The time value of the measure is counted like this:

Don't be confused by the appearance of eighth notes, their tails are connected when the notes occur together. Also, the stems of eighth notes, quarter notes, and half notes may point either upward or downward, depending on the notes' location on the staff. For a little practice try counting the time value of the following measure:

The time value in tablature is counted the same way as it is in standard musical notation.

Now that you can count the time value of notes, the next step is learning to decipher what pitch each note represents. In standard musical notation, the notes appear on a staff with five lines and four spaces. Each of these lines and spaces represents a particular note named by a letter from A to G in a scale which repeats itself.

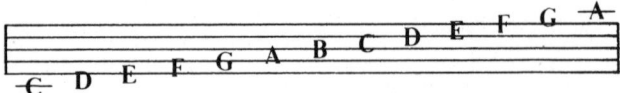

The music for the dulcimer is written in tablature which is easier to read than standard musical notation. This is because tablature indicates what fret number is to be depressed on each string. These fret numbers remain constant irregardless of the key to which the dulcimer is tuned. If standard musical notation were used, an arrangement would only work for playing a song in one key.

Music written in tablature has a slightly different appearance than music written in standard musical notation. The tablature staff contains three lines, and each of these lines represents one string. The bottom line represents the melody string. The middle line represents the middle string, and the top line represents the bass string.

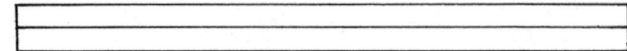

The notes used in tablature have one or more numbers at the end of the stem of each note. Quarter notes in tablature look like this:

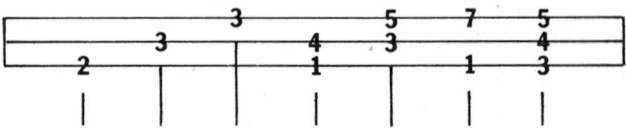

Eighth notes in tablature look like this:

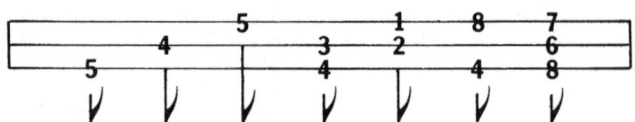

or like this when they occur together:

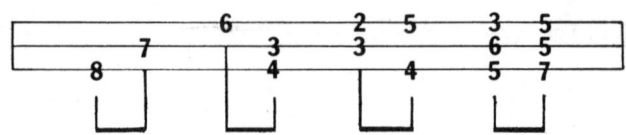

The numbers at the end of the stem of each note can vary, since they represent the frets that are to be depressed. The line on which each number appears determines which string will be fretted and picked. If no number appears on a line at the end of a stem of a note, the string is not fretted or picked.

If there is an O at the end of the stem of a note, this signifies that the string is sounded open.

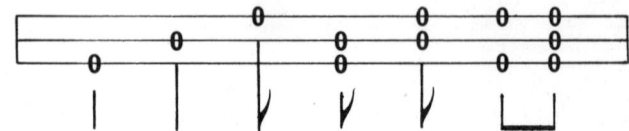

Sam Russell, dulcimer maker, Marion, Virginia, circa 1929

If two or more numbers appear over one another at the end of the stem of a note, it means that more than one string is fretted and picked simultaneously.

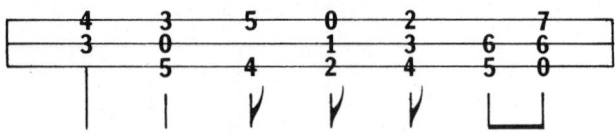

The tablature in this book is written for a dulcimer with a standard diatonic fret arrangement. Check the proportion of the lengths between the frets on your dulcimer with the fret board represented below.

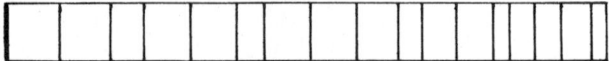

Many dulcimer makers put an extra fret between the sixth and the seventh frets. If your finger board has an extra fret there or anywhere else, simply disregard it when the music is read. These extra frets destroy the dulcimer's unique modal character.

If you have difficulty reading tablature, it might be helpful to place a piece of paper on the side of the finger board with the fret numbers listed on it, until you become familiar with this notation system.

There are a few other simple musical symbols that are used in both tablature and standard musical notation. Two vertical bars cutting the lines of the staff mean that the song has come to an end.

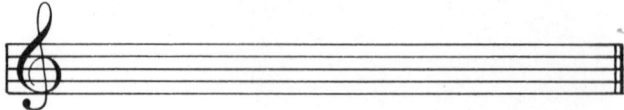

A dot after a note lengthens the relative time value of a note by a half.

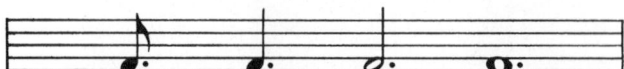

You should also be familiar with the term key signature. In standard musical notation it refers to the number of sharps ♯ and flats ♭ at the beginning of each musical staff.

Using the noter

Conventional playing position

Picks and Noters

To play the dulcimer, you should be seated on a low chair without any armrests. Place the dulcimer on your lap in a level position with the head of the instrument to your left angled slightly away from your body. A dulcimer can also be played while it is positioned on a table. This enables the table top to act as a secondary sounding board, increasing the instrument's resonance.

Traditionally two things were needed to play a dulcimer, a pick and a noter, both of which can be obtained from a variety of sources.

Originally a crow or goose quill served as a pick. A pick can be prepared from a quill by sharpening its shaft to a point. About one and a half inches above this point, slit the shaft open for about an inch upwards. This permits the feather to be strummed briskly without breaking. Although this provides a quaint pick, it is not very practical, since a quill disintegrates after several tunes. Another traditional yet more durable pick can be fashioned out of a sliver of wood such as hickory whittled down to a sharp point. Thin guitar picks are also excellent, or if you prefer to make your own plastic picks, you can cut old bleach bottles or coffee can lids into picks. An annoying clacking sound may be produced by a stiff pick. This can be eliminated by using a more flexible pick.

A noter is needed to fret the tune on the melody string. A wide variety of objects traditionally served as a noter, such as the thick end of a turkey or goose quill, a short piece of cane, or a small wooden dowel. You might even want to try using a small metal rod which will yield a whining metallic tone.

To use a noter, place it in the palm of your left hand. Your thumb applies downward pressure on it, while the forefinger guides the noter along the fret board so that it touches only the melody string. The noter should always be positioned just to the left of the fret that is to be sounded, otherwise a buzzing sound will be produced when the strings are strummed. The noter should slide up and down, never losing contact with the finger board, to produce the dulcimer's characteristic glistening tone. Your index finger can also serve as a noter. In fact, if you play in any advanced styles, where two or more strings must be fretted simultaneously, your fingers must be used to fret the strings.

Strumming

A pick strikes all the strings when a dulcimer is strummed. This is the easiest and most traditional way to play. It also effectively brings out the beauty of the drone strings, the strings other than the fretted melody string, which are constantly sounded open. There are numerous strumming variations that can be used on the dulcimer.

The first strumming sequence is for songs in 4/4 time, where the first and third beats of every measure are emphasized.

Beats
1 strum firmly toward you across all the strings
2 strum lightly away from you across all the strings
3 strum firmly toward you across all the strings
4 strum lightly away from you across all the strings

Try playing *The Old Gray Goose*, a song in 4/4 time, using this strumming sequence. If two notes are contained in one beat, the strings are struck twice in the same direction. Play only as fast as you can keep the rhythm steady. Make certain that the dulcimer is in the Ionian tuning to play this song.

The Old Gray Goose

Ionian

The one she'd been saving, (three times)
To make a feather bed.

She died last Friday, (three times)
With a pain in the back of her head.

Old gander's weeping, (three times)
Because his wife is dead.

The goslings are mourning, (three times)
Because their mother's dead.

THE OLD GRAY GOOSE
Collected, Adapted and Arranged by John Lomax & Alan Lomax
TRO—© Copyright 1934 and renewed 1962 LUDLOW MUSIC, INC., N.Y., N.Y.
Used by permission

Here is a strumming sequence for songs in 3/4 time, where the major accent falls on the first beat of each measure. To use this strumming sequence, count the beats in each measure as "one and two and three and," since the strings are struck twice on the last two beats of each measure.

Beats	
1	strum firmly toward you across all strings
and	time value left silent
2	strum lightly toward you across all strings
and	strum lightly away from you across all strings
3	strum lightly toward you across all strings
and	strum lightly away from you across all strings

After you feel comfortable with this strumming sequence, try using it on *Sweet Betsy From Pike*. At first the most important thing is to keep the rhythm flowing smoothly.

Sweet Betsy From Pike

Ionian

Chorus:
    Sing-too-rall-i-oo-ral-i-oo-ral-i-ay,
    Sing-too-rall-i-oo-ral-i-oo-ral-i-ay.

One evening quite early they camped on the Platte,
'Twas near by the road on a green shady flat;
Where Betsy, quite tired, lay down to repose,
While with wonder Ike gazed on his Pike County rose.

They swam the wide rivers and crossed the tall peaks,
And camped on the prairie for weeks upon weeks.
Starvation and cholera and hard work and slaughter,
They reached California spite of hell and high water.

Out on the prairie one bright starry night
They broke the whisky and Betsy got tight,
She sang and she shouted and danced o'er the plain,
And showed her bare arse to the whole wagon train.

The Injuns came down in a wild yelling horde,
And Betsy was skeered they would scalp her adored;
Behind the front wagon wheel Betsy did crawl,
And there she fought the Injuns with musket and ball.

The alkali desert was burning and bare,
And Isaac's soul shrank from the death that lurked there:
"Dear old Pike County, I'll go back to you."
Says Betsy, "You'll go by yourself if you do."

They soon reached the desert, where Betsy gave out,
And down in the sand she lay rolling about;
While Ike in great terror looked on in surprise,
Saying, "Betsy, get up, you'll get sand in your eyes."

Sweet Betsy got up in a great deal of pain
And declared she'd go back to Pike County again;
Then Ike heaved a sigh and they fondly embraced,
And she traveled along with his arm round her waist.

    SWEET BETSY FROM PIKE
    Collected, Adapted and Arranged by John Lomax & Alan Lomax
    TRO—© Copyright 1934 and renewed 1962 LUDLOW MUSIC, INC., N.Y., N.Y.
                Used by permission

They went to Salt Lake to inquire the way,
And Brigham declared that sweet Betsy should stay;
But Betsy got frightened and ran like a deer,
While Brigham stood pawing the earth like a steer.

The wagon tipped over with a terrible crash,
And out on the prairie rolled all sorts of trash;
A few little baby clothes done up with care
Looked rather suspicious, but it was all on the square.

One morning they climbed a very high hill,
And with wonder looked down on old Placerville;
Ike shouted and said, as he cast his eyes down,
"Sweet Betsy, my darling, we've got to Hangtown."

Long Ike and sweet Betsy attended a dance,
Where Ike wore a pair of his Pike County pants;
Sweet Betsy was covered with ribbons and rings,
Said Ike, "You're an angel, but where are your wings?"

A miner said, "Betsy, will you dance with me?"
"I will that, old hoss, if you don't make too free;
But don't dance me hard. Do you want to know why?
Doggone ye, I'm chock-full of strong alkali."

Long Ike and sweet Betsy got married of course,
But Ike, getting jealous, obtained a divorce;
And Betsy, well satisfied, said with a shout,
"Good-by, you big lummox, I'm glad you backed out."

Participants in American Folk Song Festival, circa 1950

The next few songs presented here are in the four modes most commonly used in folk music: the Ionian, Aeolian, Dorian, and Mixolydian modes. These songs will give you practice tuning to different modes.

Here are a few subtle techniques to vary your strumming style. The angle your pick strikes the strings enables you to emphasize the drone strings or melody string. Striking the strings at different locations is another variation, the closer they are struck toward the bridge, the tinnier their tone.

Pretty Polly

Dorian

PRETTY POLLY
Collected, Adapted and Arranged by John Lomax & Alan Lomax
TRO—© Copyright 1941 and renewed 1969 LUDLOW MUSIC, INC., N.Y., N.Y.
Used by permission

She got up behind him and away they did go,
Over the hills to the valleys below.

They went a little farther and what did they spy?
A new-dug grave and a spade lying by.

"Willie, O Willie, I'm afraid of your way,
I'm afraid you will lead my poor body astray."

"Pretty Polly, pretty Polly, you're thinking just right,
I dug on your grave the best part of last night."

He threw her onto the ground, and she broke into tears,
She threw her arms around him and trembled with fear.

"O Willie, please Willie, please spare my sweet life,
How can you kill a girl that was to be your wife?"

"There's no time to talk now, there's no time to stand,"
He drew out his knife all in his right hand.

He stabbed her to the heart, her heart's blood it did flow,
And into the grave pretty Polly did go.

He threw a little dirt over her and started for home,
Leaving no one behind but the wild birds to mourn.

A debt to the devil poor Willie must pay,
For killing pretty Polly and running away.

A group of mountain musicians including Bunyan Day, kin of the noted Days of Rowan County, circa 1925

Drill Ye Tarriers

Aeolian

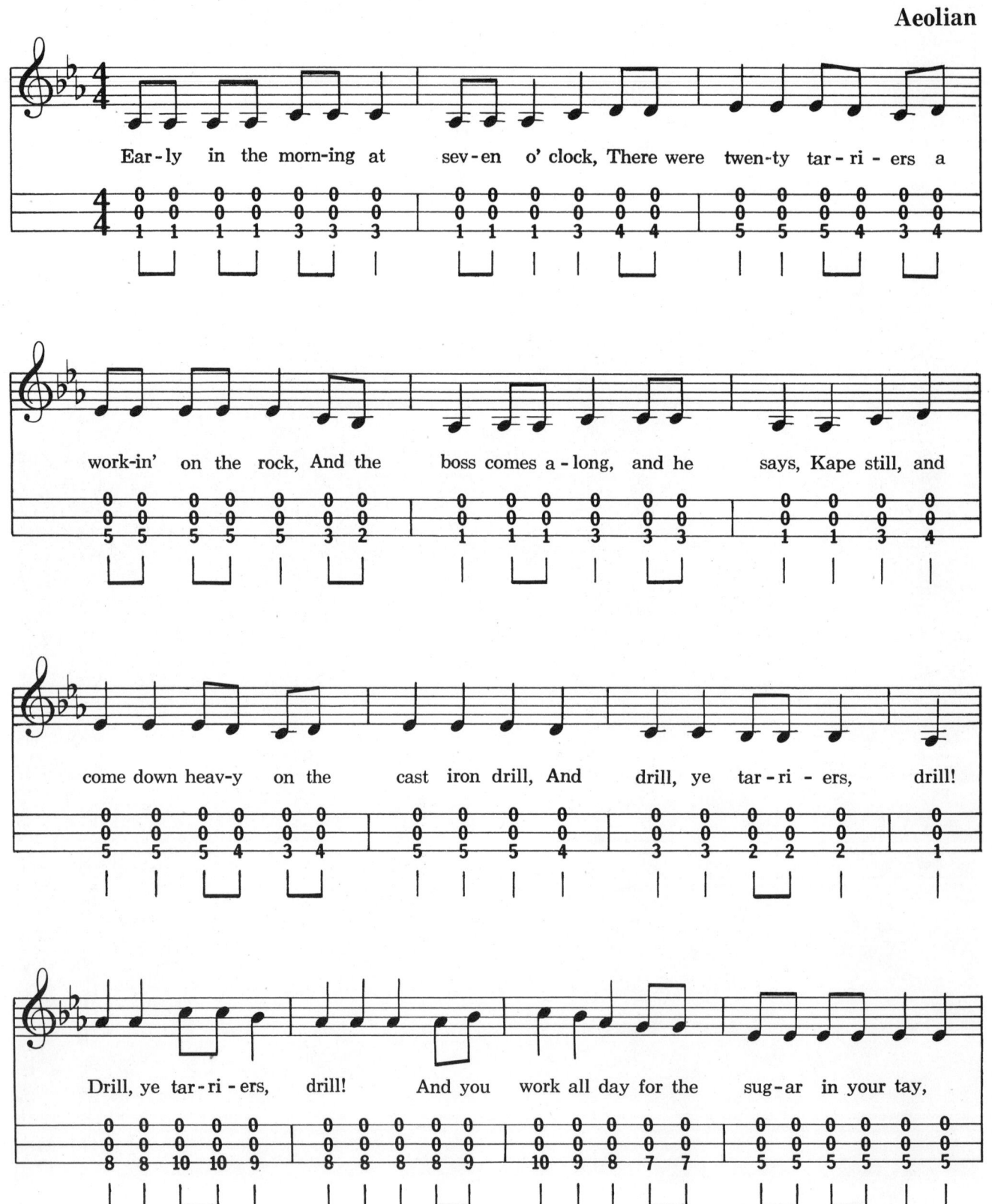

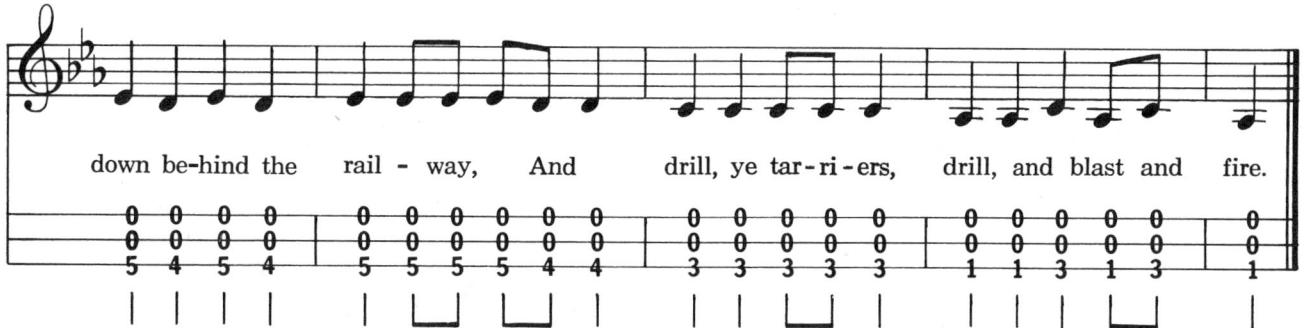

The boss was a fine man down to the ground
And he married a lady six feet 'round;
She baked good bread, and she baked it well,
But she baked it hard as the holes of hell!

Now the new foreman was Jean McCann;
By God, he was a blamed mean man!
Last week a premature blast went off,
And a mile in the air went big Jim Goff.

The next time pay day came around,
Jim Goff a dollar short was found.
When he asked what for, came this reply:
"You were docked for the time you were up in the sky."

Unidentified dulcimer player, circa 1930

Old Joe Clark

Mixolydian

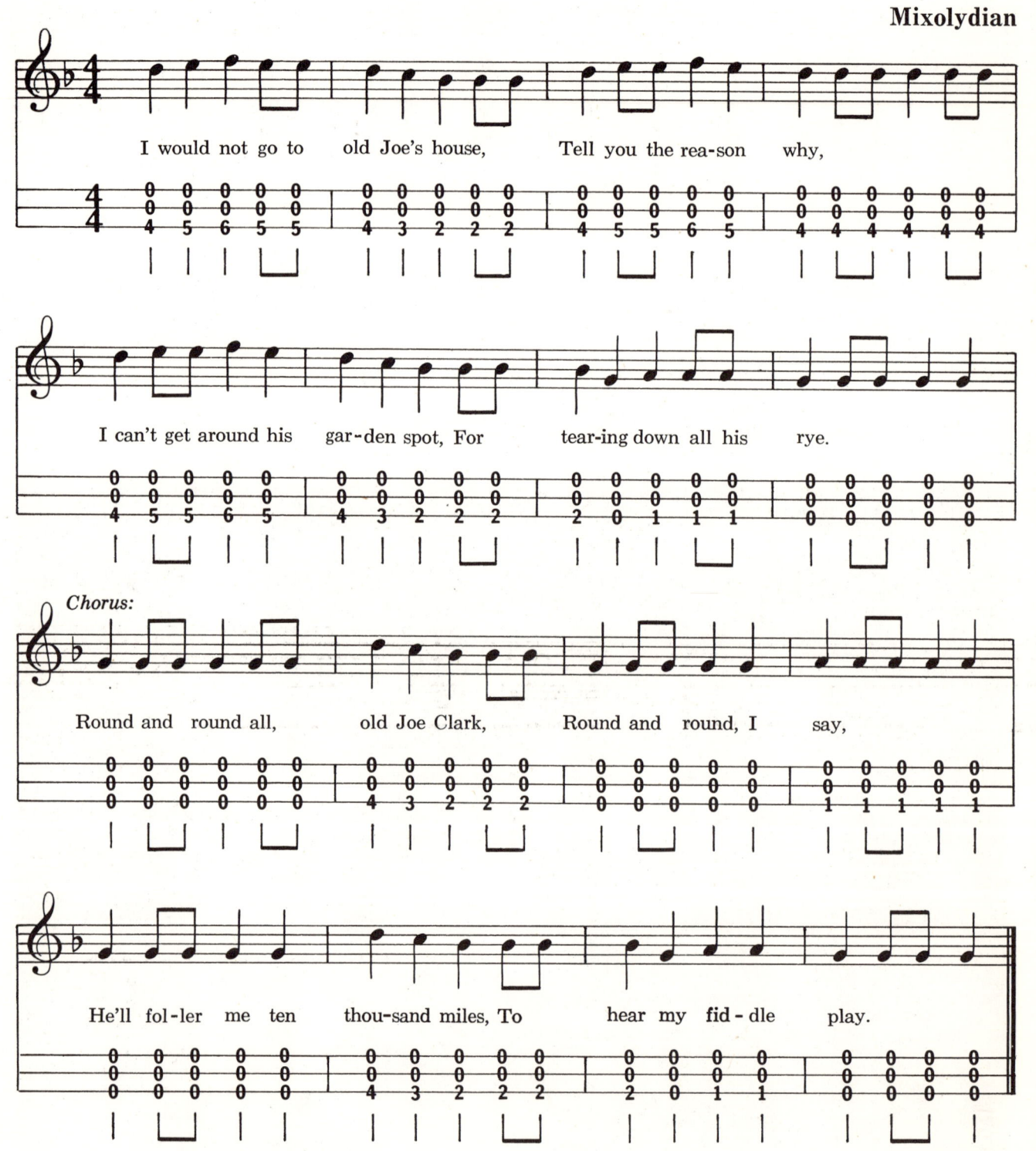

OLD JOE CLARK
Collected, Adapted and Arranged by John Lomax & Alan Lomax
TRO—© Copyright 1934 and renewed 1962 LUDLOW MUSIC, INC., N.Y., N.Y.
Used by permission

Old Joe's got an old red cow,
I know her by the bell.
If she ever gits in my cornfield,
I'll shoot her shore as Hell.

Chorus:
Round and round all, old Joe Clark,
Round and round, I say,
Round and round, old Joe Clark,
I ain't got long to stay.

I went up to old Joe's house,
Old Joe wasn't home;
I eat up all of his ham meat
And throwed away the bone.

Chorus:
Fare you well, old Joe Clark,
Good-by, Betty Brown,
Fare you well, old Joe Clark,
Fare you well, I'm gone.

I went down to old Joe Clark's,
Old Joe wasn't home;
Jumped in bed with old Joe's wife
And broke her tucking comb.

I won't go down to old Joe's house,
I've told you here before;
He fed me in a hog-trough
And I won't go there any more.

Sixteen horses in my team,
And the leaders, they are blind;
And every time the sun goes down,
There's a pretty gal on my mind.

Eighteen miles of mountain road
And fifteen miles of sand;
If I ever travel this road again,
I'll be a married man.

Never got no money,
Got no place to stay,
Got no place to lay my head,
Chicken's a-crowin' for day.

I wish I was an apple
A-hanging on yonder's tree—
Ev'ry time a pretty gal passed
She'd take a bite of me.

Wish I was a sugar tree,
Standing in the middle of some town
Ev'ry time a pretty gal passed,
I'd shake some sugar down.

Wish I had a nickel,
Wish I had a dime,
Wish I had a pretty lil gal,
For to kiss her an' call her mine.

Wish I was in Tennessee,
Settin' in a big armcheer,
One arm round my whisky jug,
The other round my dear.

I climbed up the oak tree,
She climbed up the gum;
Never saw a pretty lil gal,
But what I loved her some.

When I was a little girl
I used to play with toys;
But now I am a bigger girl
I'd rather play with boys.

When I was a little boy
I used to want a knife;
But now I am a bigger boy
All I want is a wife.

Unidentified group of musicians, circa 1930

John Henry

Mixolydian

JOHN HENRY
Collected, Adapted and Arranged by John Lomax & Alan Lomax
TRO—© Copyright 1941 and renewed 1969 LUDLOW MUSIC, INC., N.Y., N.Y.
Used by permission

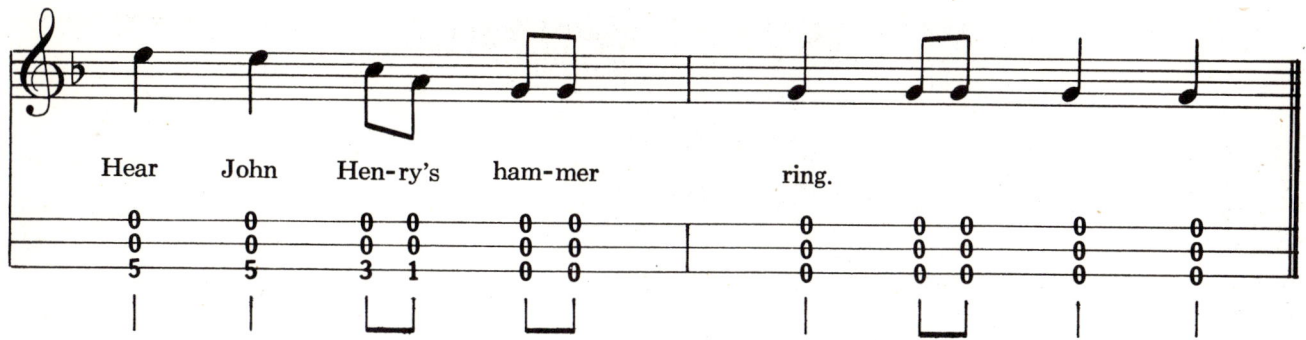

John Henry told his old lady,
"Will you fix my supper soon?
Got ninety miles o' track I've got to line,
Got to line it by the light of the moon, oh, Lawdy,
Line it by the light o' the moon."

John Henry had a little baby,
He could hold him out in his hand;
But the last word I heard that po' child say,
"My dad is a steel-drivin' man, oh, Lawdy,
Daddy is a steel-drivin' man."

John Henry told his old capt'in,
Said, "A man ain't nothin' but a man,
Before I let yo' steel gang down
I will die with the hammer in my hand, oh, Lawdy,
Die with the hammer in my hand."

John Henry told his capt'in,
"Next time you go to town
A-jes' bring me back a ten-pound maul
Fer to beat yo' steel-drivin' down, oh, Lawdy,
Beat yo' steel-drivin' down."

John Henry had a old lady,
An' her name was Polly Ann.
John Henry tuck sick an' he had to go to bed;
Pauline drove steel like a man, oh, Lawdy,
P'line drove steel like a man.

John Henry had a old lady,
An' the dress she wo' was red;
Well, she started up the track an' she never looked back,
"Gwine where my man fell dead, oh, Lawdy,
Where my man fell dead."

Well, they taken John Henry to Wash'n'ton,
An' they bury him in the san',
There's people from the East an' there's people from the West
Come to see such a steel-drivin' man, oh, Lawdy,
See such a steel-drivin' man.

Well, some say he's fum England,
Well, an' some say he's fum Spain,
But I say he's nothin' but a Lou's'ana man,
Jes' the leader of a steel-drivin' gang, oh, Lawdy,
Leader of a steel-drivin' gang.

Unidentified group of musicians, circa 1930

Will Singleton, dulcimer maker, Viper, Kentucky, circa 1929

Scarborough Fair

Dorian

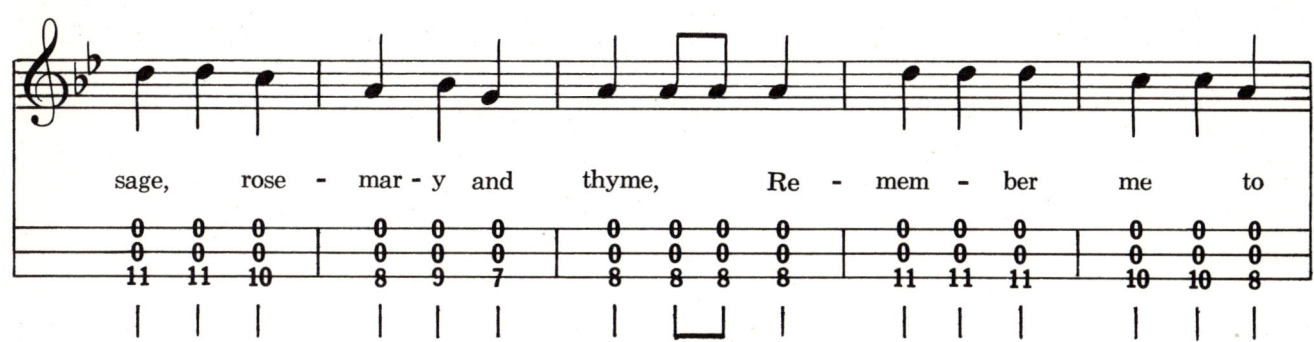

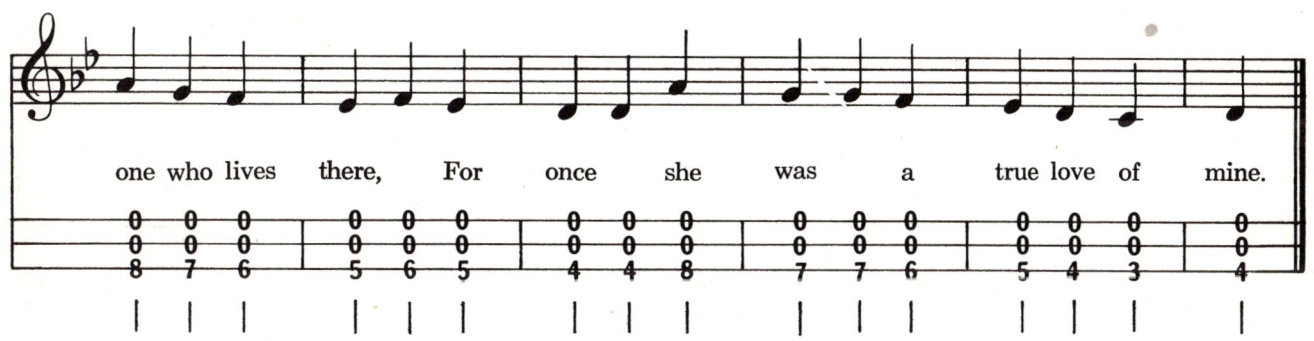

Tell her to plow it with horses three,
Parsley, sage, rosemary and thyme,
And sow it all over with spices for me,
And then she'll be a true love of mine.

Tell her to gath'r it in one day's span,
Parsley, sage, rosemary and thyme,
And then, O then, I'll be her true man,
And then she'll be a true love of mine.

Tell her to sew me a plain, good shirt,
Parsley, sage, rosemary and thyme,
Without no seam nor a fancy work,
And then she'll be a true love of mine.

Tell her to find me an acre of ground,
Parsley, sage, rosemary and thyme,
Then she must plant it all round, all round,
And then she'll be a true love of mine.

If you're going to Scarborough Fair,
Parsley, sage, rosemary and thyme,
Remember me to one who lives there,
I wish she'd be a true love of mine.

OLD DAN TUCKER
Collected, Adapted and Arranged by John Lomax & Alan Lomax
TRO—© Copyright 1934 and renewed 1962 LUDLOW MUSIC, INC., N.Y., N.Y.
Used by permission

"Miss Tucker she went out one day,
To ride with Dan in a one horse sleigh.
De sleigh was broke, and de horse was blind—
Miss Tucker she got left behind.
   Git out o' the way, etc.

"As I come down de new cut road,
I spied de peckerwood and de toad,
And every time de toad would jump
De peckerwood hopped upon de stump.
   Git out o' the way, etc.

"And next upon de gravel road,
I met Br'er Tarrypin and Br'er Toad.
And every time Br'er Toad would sing
Br'er Tarrypin cut de pigeon wing.
   Git out o' the way, etc.

"Ole Dan and me we did fall out,
And what d'ye reckon it was about?
He trod on my corn and I kicked him on the shins;
That's jest the way this row begins.
   Git out o' the way, etc.

"If Ole Dan he had corn to buy,
He'd mo'n and wipe his weepin' eye;
But when Ole Dan had corn to sell,
He was as sassy as all hell.
   Git out o' the way, etc.

Old Timers Day, July 4, 1934, Brasstown, North Carolina. John Jacob Niles playing dulcimer

Bowing

You might want to try bowing your dulcimer. Although this was a little used technique, it can effectively bring out the dulcimer's rich, full tone. There is really no difference between bowing and strumming the dulcimer, except that the strings are sounded with a bow instead of a pick. The bow crosses all the strings once each beat. All you need to bow a dulcimer is a violin bow and plenty of rosin. The picture of Mrs. Leah Smith suggests a convenient way to hold the dulcimer while it is being bowed.

Mrs. Leah Smith of Greasy Creek, Kentucky on her front porch bowing the dulcimer, circa 1940

Picking

Aside from the strumming styles presented so far, a dulcimer's strings can also be picked individually with the fingers. Although picking destroys the dulcimer's characteristic droning tone, it can add much versatility to your playing style. Most commonly when picking the strings, the thumb strikes the melody string, while the index finger picks the middle string and the middle finger picks the bass string.

Picking sequences are determined by the time signature of a song. Two common picking sequences are provided here. The first is for songs in 4/4 time:

Beats

1 Thumb picks the melody string away from you
2 Index finger picks the middle string toward you
3 Middle finger picks the bass string toward you or for variation the thumb picks the melody string away from you
4 Index finger picks the middle string toward you

Remember that in 4/4 time the melody string or all the strings are usually struck with the thumb on the first and third beats of each measure, the accented beats in 4/4 time. As you practice this sequence, try counting the beats. After you become proficient with this sequence, try using it on the following song.

Picking the strings

Long Long Ago

Ionian

65

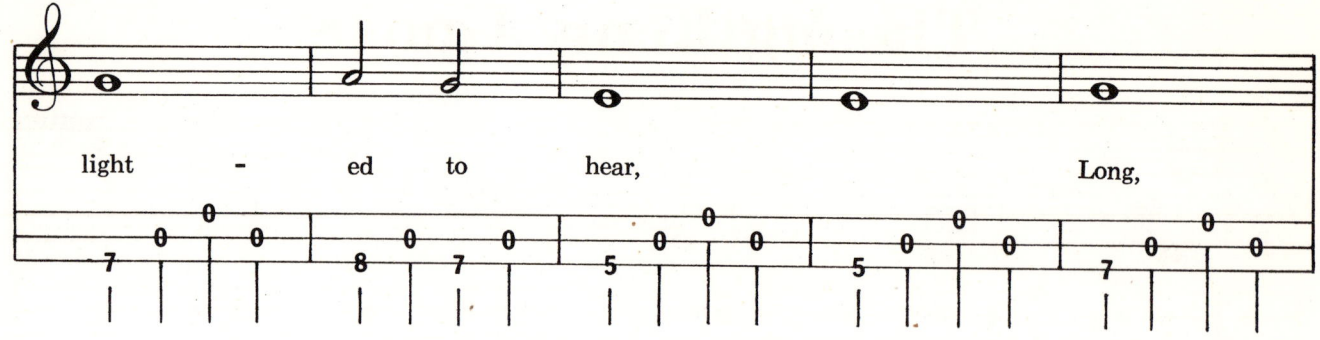

Tho' by your kindness my fond hopes were rais'd,
Long, long ago, Long, long ago,
You by more eloquent lips have been prais'd,
Long, long ago, long ago.

Do you remember the path where we met,
Long, long ago, Long, long ago?
Ah, yes, you told me you ne'er would forget,
Long, long ago, long ago.

Jean Thomas, founder of the American Folk Song Festival, along with participants of the festival

The Old Gray Goose

Ionian

The one she'd been saving, (three times)
To make a feather bed.

She died last Friday, (three times)
With a pain in the back of her head.

Old gander's weeping, (three times)
Because his wife is dead.

The goslings are mourning, (three times)
Because their mother's dead.

THE OLD GRAY GOOSE
Collected, Adapted and Arranged by John Lomax & Alan Lomax
TRO—© Copyright 1934 and renewed 1962 LUDLOW MUSIC, INC., N.Y., N.Y.
Used by permission

Here is a useful picking sequence for songs in 3/4 time:

Beats
1 Thumb picks the melody string away from you
2 Index finger picks the middle string toward you
3 Middle finger picks the bass string toward you or for variation the thumb picks the melody string away from you while the middle finger simultaneously picks the bass string toward you

In 3/4 time the melody string or all of the strings are usually struck with the thumb on the first beat of each measure, since this is the accented beat of the measure. *Sumer Is Icumen In*, the following song, uses the picking sequence just described.

These two picking sequences are only suggestive of the numerous ones that can be used. Remember when experimenting with different picking sequences that the time signature of a song usually determines which sequence is best suited to it.

Sumer Is Icumen In

Ionian

Chord Formation

Many fine dulcimer instrumentalists fret only the melody string when they play. Many songs sound better played in this style than in any other. However, chords can be used to create more complicated arrangements. If you wish to use chords, it is first best to gain an understanding of what a chord consists of before you learn how they are used in relationship with each other.

Basically a chord is the simultaneous voicing of several notes which produces a concordant or dissonant harmonic relationship. Many existing chords can't be sounded on a dulcimer, which has only a seven note scale on its diatonically fretted finger board. However, there are numerous chords and a number of variations of these same chords or inversions that can be produced on the dulcimer.

Most dulcimer chords are quite simple in construction. They are the voicing of three notes, called a triad, possessing certain tonal relationships. In the most common chord formation, the first note of a chord is called the root or tonic note. There is also a major third, a note which is

Chording the strings

three notes above the root note counting the root note as one; and a perfect fifth, a note which is five notes above the root note counting the root note as one. The root note is the most important note of the chord, since all of the other notes in a chord are determined from its location. A chord is always named by the note on which the root or tonic note of the chord falls. For instance, if the root or tonic note of a chord falls on a C, the chord is called a C chord.

To form a C chord, first locate a C on the fret board. To find the major third, count up three notes above the C, counting C as the first note: C, D, E. This makes E the major third. To locate the perfect fifth, count up five notes from the root of the chord: C, D, E, F, G. This makes G the perfect fifth. These three notes are then fretted on separate strings to create this chord.

If the strings on which the third and fifth are located aren't tuned to the same pitch as the string on which the tonic note is located, the easiest way to find the strings tonal relationships to each other is to refer to the tuning chart. From there you can easily determine where the strings must be fretted to create chords.

Although most dulcimer chords are created as just described, there are several possible variations to this scheme. The first chord formation is only valid for creating major chords, but it is also possible to form minor chords. Only one element distinguishes a minor chord from a major chord. In a major chord the third is three full notes above the root of the chord counting the root note as one, while in a minor chord the third is separated from the root of the chord by only two and a half notes counting the root note as one. The difference in a chord's thirds appreciably alters the sound of the chord so that it may be classified as either minor or major.

There is also the possibility of forming full or open minor and major chords. A full major or minor chord contains a root, a major or minor third, and a perfect fifth. Open chords contain variations of the notes in full chords. To form an open major chord, sound the tonic note. The third and/or fifth of the chord may be omitted. The only note that must necessarily be played in an open major chord is the tonic note, since this note determines which chord you are playing. However, to form an open minor chord, you must sound the tonic note and a minor third. If the minor third isn't sounded, the chord is indistinguishable from a major chord.

Using Chords

Now that you understand chord formation, you are ready to learn how chords are used in conjunction with one another to form chordal progressions.

Most folk songs use only I, IV, V, or tonic, subdominant, dominant chords to create chordal progressions.

The I chord is always named by the first note or keynote of the modal scale to which the dulcimer is tuned. The names of the IV and V chords are found by counting up four and five notes from the first note or keynote of the modal scale, which is counted as one.

For instance, this is how you would find the names of the I, IV, and V chords on a dulcimer tuned to the Ionian mode in the key of C. The I chord would be C, since this is the keynote or first note of this modal scale. To find the names of the IV and V chords, count up four and five notes respectively from C, counting C as the first note. This will give you the notes F and G, the names of the IV and V chords.

Aside from the I, IV, V chords, the VI chord, the relative minor of any major key, is occasionally used. The VI chord can replace the I chord in any major key for variety. The name of the VI chord is found by counting up six notes from the first note or keynote of any modal scale, which is counted as one.

Chords are fretted with whatever fingers can reach the notes most easily. This usually includes all but the little finger. Remember that chords are not normally used throughout an entire song, but only for emphasis.

The chart below contains the names of the I, IV, V chords for all modes tuned to their traditional key:

MODE	KEY	I	IV	V CHORDS
Ionian	C	C	F	G
Dorian	D	D	G	A
Phrygian	E	E	A	B
Lydian	F	F	B♭	C
Mixolydian	G	G	C	D
Aeolian	A	A	D	E
Locrian	B	B	E	F

The following songs are provided to give you an idea of how chords can be used.

Chord Charts

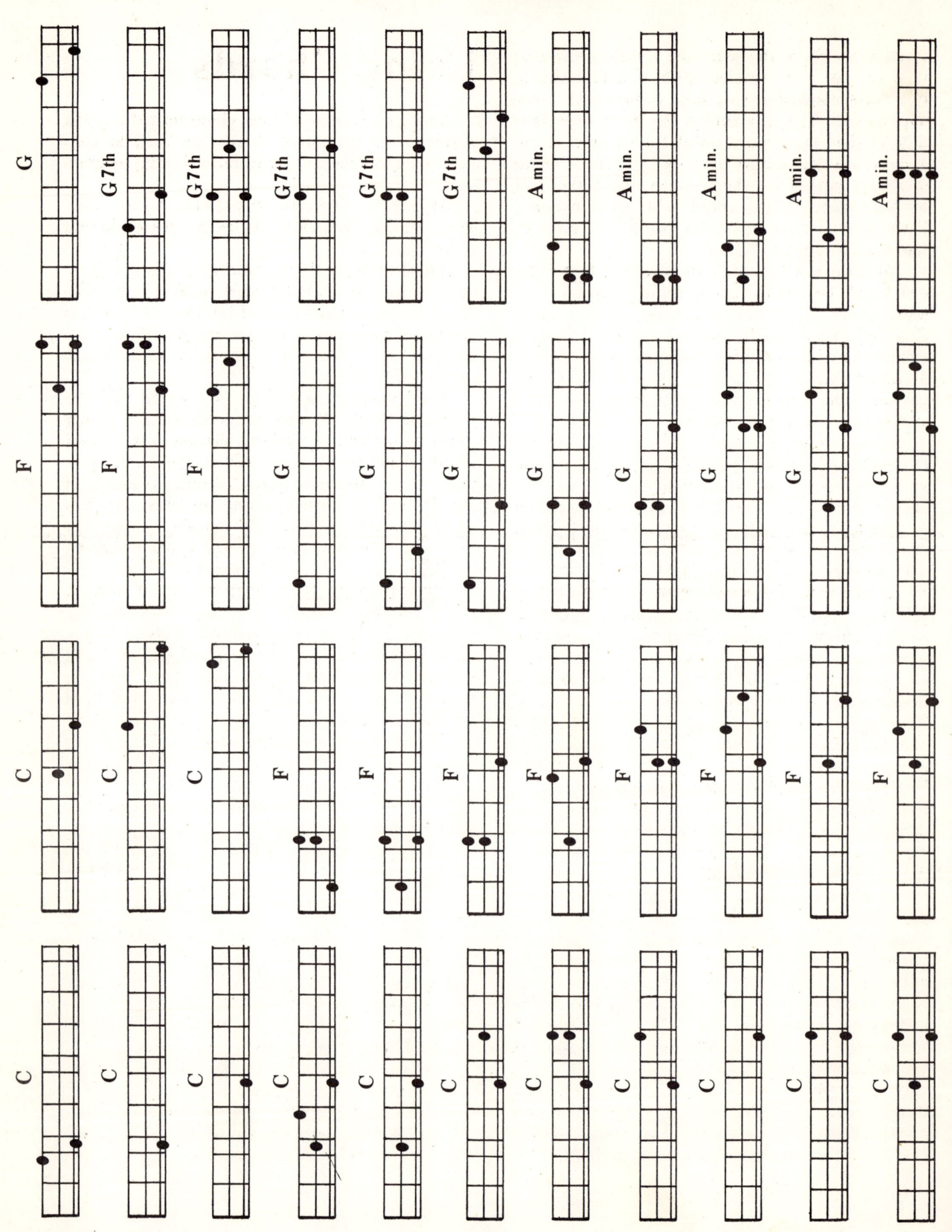

Ionian

Chord Charts

Mixolydian   Aeolian

The Old Gray Goose

Ionian

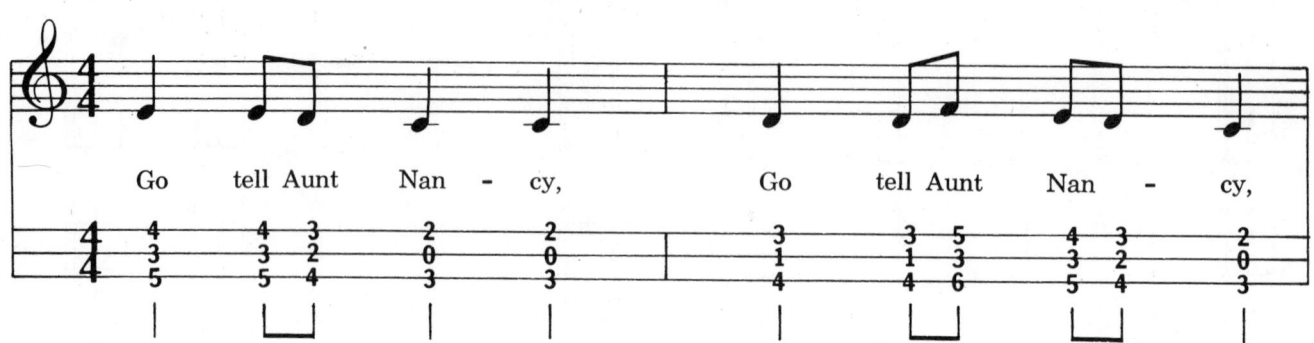

The one she'd been saving, (three times)
To make a feather bed.

She died last Friday, (three times)
With a pain in the back of her head.

Old gander's weeping, (three times)
Because his wife is dead.

The goslings are mourning, (three times)
Because their mother's dead.

THE OLD GRAY GOOSE
Collected, Adapted and Arranged by John Lomax & Alan Lomax
TRO—© Copyright 1934 and renewed 1962 LUDLOW MUSIC, INC., N.Y., N.Y.
Used by permission

Amazing Grace

Ionian

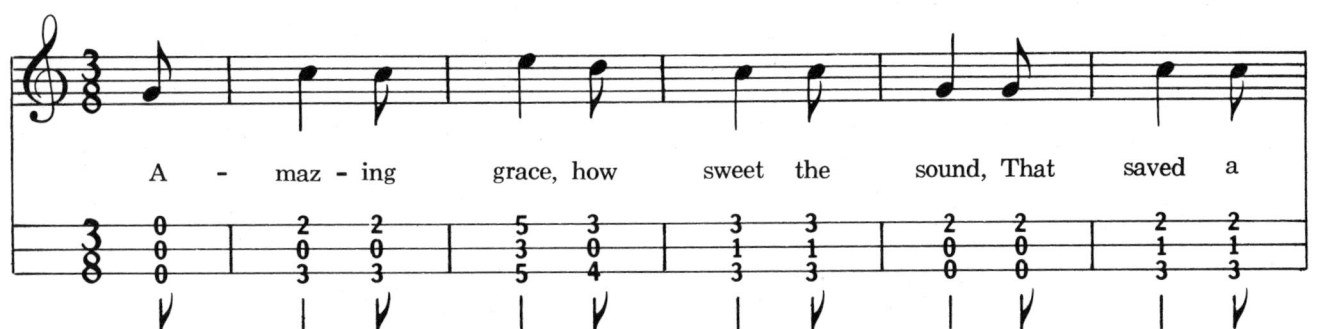

Through many dangers, toils, and snares,
I have already come;
'Tis grace that brought me safe this far,
And grace will lead me home.

'Twas grace that taught my heart to fear,
And grace my fears relieved;
How precious did that grace appear,
The hour I first believed!

AMAZING GRACE
    Collected, Adapted and Arranged by John Lomax & Alan Lomax
    TRO—© Copyright 1934 and renewed 1962 LUDLOW MUSIC, INC., N.Y., N.Y.
                                        Used by permission

Counter Melodies

A counter melody is a simple technique used to enhance the melody of a song. To play a counter melody, fret the melody on the first string as usual, while another string is simultaneously fretted separated from the melody note on the first string by a third. The location of the third is found exactly as it was in chord formation. The note played on the first string acts as the root and is counted as one when locating the third. The third is separated from the root note by either two and a half notes if it is minor or by three notes if it is major, depending on the intervals between the frets. Counter melodies are most easily fretted using the thumb and index or middle finger. The songs that follow use counter melodies and variations of counter melodies.

The Old Gray Goose

Ionian

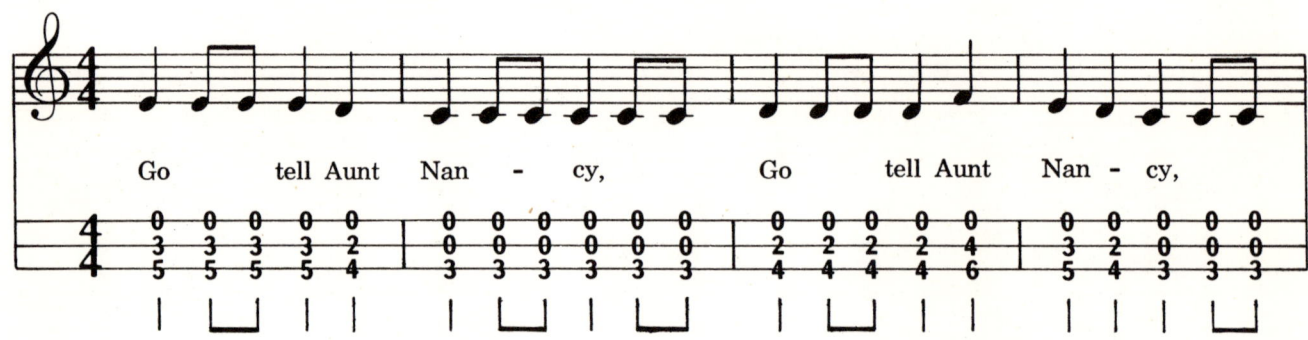

The one she'd been saving, (three times)
To make a feather bed.

She died last Friday, (three times)
With a pain in the back of her head.

Old gander's weeping, (three times)
Because his wife is dead.

The goslings are mourning, (three times)
Because their mother's dead.

THE OLD GRAY GOOSE
Collected, Adapted and Arranged by John Lomax & Alan Lomax
TRO—© Copyright 1934 and renewed 1962 LUDLOW MUSIC, INC., N.Y., N.Y.
Used by permission

Frank Ritchie, Viper, Kentucky, circa 1929

Hush Li'l Baby

Ionian

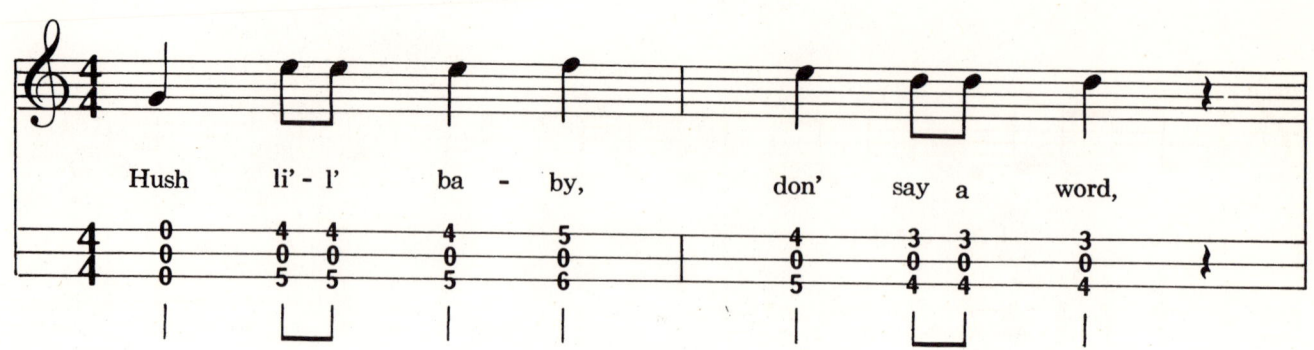

If that mockin' bird don' sing,
Mamma's gonna buy you a diamond ring.

If that diamond ring turn brass,
Mamma's gonna buy you a lookin' glass.

If that lookin' glass gets broke,
Mamma's gonna buy you a billygoat.

If that billygoat won' pull,
Mamma's gonna buy you a cart and bull.

If that cart and bull turn over,
Mamma's gonna buy you a dog named Rover.

If that dog named Rover won' bark,
Mamma's gonna buy you a horse and cart.

If that horse and cart fall down,
You'll be the sweetest girl in town.

HUSH, LI'L BABY
Collected, Adapted and Arranged by John Lomax & Alan Lomax
TRO—© Copyright 1941 and renewed 1969 LUDLOW MUSIC, INC., N.Y., N.Y.
Used by permission

The Old Gray Goose

Ionian

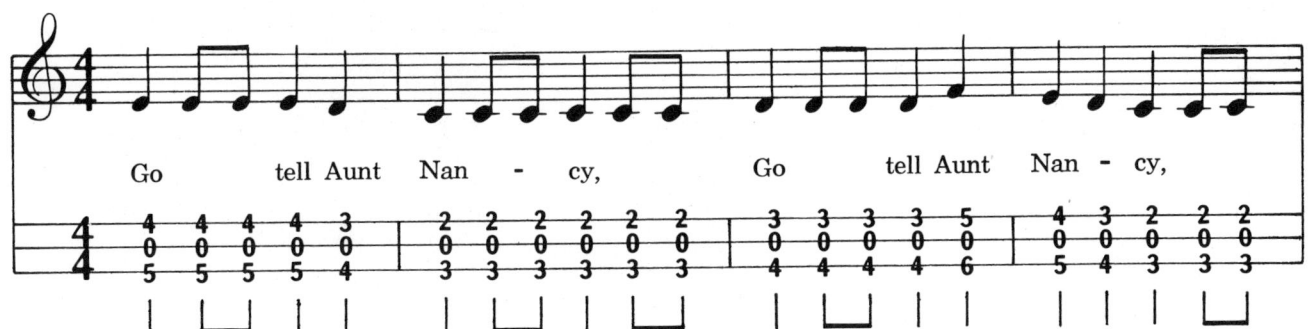

The one she'd been saving, (three times)
To make a feather bed.

She died last Friday, (three times)
With a pain in the back of her head.

Old gander's weeping, (three times)
Because his wife is dead.

The goslings are mourning, (three times)
Because their mother's dead.

THE OLD GRAY GOOSE
Collected, Adapted and Arranged by John Lomax & Alan Lomax
TRO—© Copyright 1934 and renewed 1962 LUDLOW MUSIC, INC., N.Y., N.Y.
Used by permission

Unidentified dulcimer player, circa 1930

Shenandoah

Ionian

Missouri she's a mighty river, A-way ay, you rolling river. The Indians camp along its borders, A-ha, I'm bound away 'Cross the wide Missouri.

The white man loved an Indian maiden,
With notions his canoe was laden.

O Shenandoah, I love your daughter,
I've crossed for her the rolling water.

The chief, he made an awful holler,
He turned away the trader's dollars.

Along there came a Yankee skipper,
He winked at her and tipped his flipper.

He sold the chief some fire water,
He got him drunk and stole his daughter.

O Shenandoah, I long to hear you,
Come back across the rolling water.

(Each verse carries the same refrain as the first.)

SHENANDOAH
Collected, Adapted and Arranged by John Lomax & Alan Lomax
TRO—© Copyright 1934 and renewed 1962 LUDLOW MUSIC, INC., N.Y., N.Y.
Used by permission

Tom Dooley

Ionian

Chorus:
Hang down your head, Tom Dooley,
Hang down your head and cry,
Hang down your head, Tom Dooley,
Poor boy, you're bound to die.

Chorus:
I met her on the mountain,
I swore she'd be my wife,
I met her on the mountain,
And I stabbed her with my knife.

This time tomorrow,
Reckon where I'll be,
Down in some lonesome valley
A-hangin' on a white-oak tree.

Chorus:
I had my trial at Wilksboro,'
And what d'you reckon they done?
They bound me over to Statesville
And that's where I'll be hung.

The limb a-bein' oak, boys,
The rope a-bein' strong,
Bow down your head, Tom Dooley,
You know you're gonna be hung.

Chorus:
Pappy, O pappy,
What shall I do?
I lost all my money
And killed poor Laurie, too.

Mammy, O mammy,
Don't you weep or cry,
I've killed poor Laurie Foster
And you know I'm bound to die.

Chorus:
O what my mammy told me,
Is about to come to pass,
Red whisky and pretty women,
Would be my ruin at last.

TOM DOOLEY
Words & Music collected, adapted and arranged by Frank Warner, John Lomax & Alan Lomax
TRO—© Copyright 1947 (renewed 1975) and 1958 LUDLOW MUSIC, INC., N.Y., N.Y.
Used by permission

Trio with dulcimer, Homeplace, Kentucky. Left to right: Unidentified, Lula Hole, Arlie Fay Allen, circa 1929

Greensleeves

Aeolian

I have been ready at your hand,
To grant whatever you would crave;
I have both waged life and land,
Your love and good-will for to have.

If you intend thus to disdain,
It does the more enrapture me,
And even so, I still remain
A lover in captivity.

My men were clothed all in green,
And they did ever wait on thee;
All this was gallant to be seen;
And yet thou wouldst not love me.

Thou couldst desire no earthly thing,
But still thou hadst it readily.
Thy music still to play and sing;
And yet thou wouldst not love me.

Well, I will pray to God on high,
That thou my constancy mayst see,
And that yet once before I die,
Thou wilt vouchsafe to love me.

Ah, Greensleeves, now farewell, adieu,
To God I pray to prosper thee,
For I am still thy lover true,
Come once again and love me.

Bristol Taylor, dulcimer maker, Berea, Kentucky, circa 1929

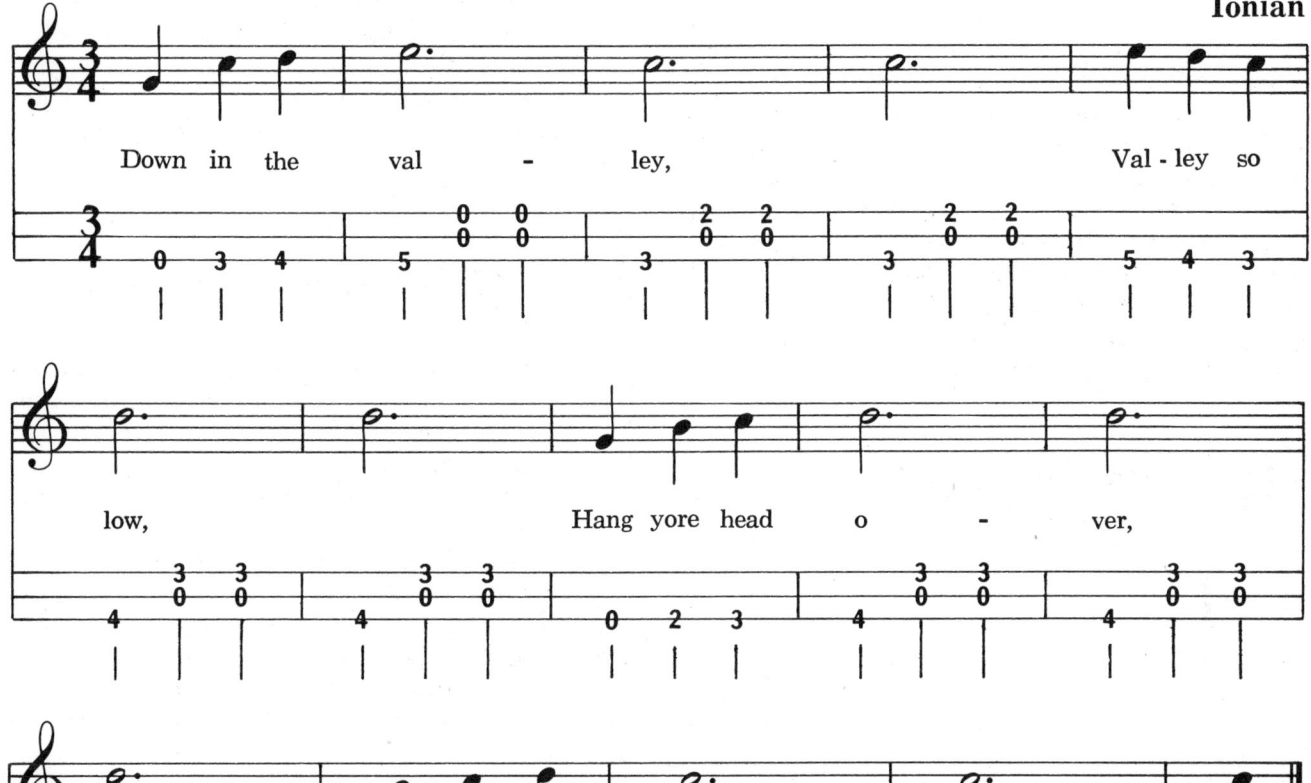

If you don't love me,
Love whom you please,
But throw yore arms round me,
Give my heart ease.
Give my heart ease, dear,
Give my heart ease,
Throw yore arms round me,
Give my heart ease.

Down in the valley
Walking between,
Telling our story,
Here's what it sings—
Roses of sunshine,
Vi'lets of dew,
Angels in heaven,
Knows I love you.

Build me a castle,
Forty feet high,
So I can see her
As she goes by.
As she goes by, dear,
As she goes by,
So I can see her,
As she goes by.

Bird in a cage, love,
Bird in a cage,
Dying for freedom,
Ever a slave.
Ever a slave, dear,
Ever a slave,
Dying for freedom,
Ever a slave.

Write me a letter;
Send it by mail;
And back it in care of
The Barbourville jail.
Barbourville jail, love,
Barbourville jail,
And back it in care of
The Barbourville jail.

DOWN IN THE VALLEY
Collected, Adapted and Arranged by John Lomax & Alan Lomax
TRO—© Copyright 1934 and renewed 1962 LUDLOW MUSIC, INC., N.Y., N.Y.
Used by permission

Bending Notes

Bending a note raises a string's pitch about half a tone and produces a sharp. Although this embellishment takes the dulcimer out of the mode to which it is tuned, it can add much to a melodic passage. To bend a note, push a string slightly to the side wherever it is normally fretted with your finger or noter. The farther the string is pushed, the higher its tone is raised. When bending a note, make certain that you have a good grip on the string, since it can be rather elusive. Bent notes are used for occasional emphasis.

Hammering On

Hammering on a string results in a note being sounded between picking actions. To hammer on a string, the index finger or noter is brought down sharply on a string a split second before it is sounded. This technique sounds best when it is employed sparingly. A sound resembling hammering on can also be produced by quick slides with a noter.

Tremolo

Tremolo is an excellent technique for creating an air of mystery in a song. To produce a tremolo effect, wiggle your finger or noter back and forth on a string's normal fretting position immediately after the string has been struck.

Pulling Off

Pulling off a note involves sounding two notes on the same string almost simultaneously. To pull off a note, fret one string at two different locations. Immediately after the string is struck, the finger closest to the picking action is pulled off toward you, leaving the string fretted farther up the finger board. After pulling off the first finger, the string might be sounded open, if it was initially fretted in only one location.

For example, if you wish to achieve the tonal effect of a string being sounded on the fifth and the second fret between two picking actions, with two fingers, fret one string on the second and fifth frets. Immediately after the string is strummed, the finger on the fifth fret would be pulled off, while the finger on the second fret would remain, producing two distinct tones on the same string almost simultaneously. Pulling off is used mainly for variety.

Harmonics

Harmonics are clear, bell-like tones emitted when a string is fretted and picked, using a special technique, at points which divide the distance between the nut and the bridge in equal proportions. The location of the first harmonic is found by dividing the length from the nut to the bridge in half which places the first or main harmonic under the seventh fret. To find the next two harmonics, divide the length between the nut and the bridge in three equal proportions. This places harmonics under the fourth and eleventh frets. Although other harmonics can be found similarly, their tone will not be as clear or as strong as these first three harmonics.

To sound a harmonic, press a string lightly over one of the specified frets. Then release the string quickly and pluck it at that instant. The bell-like tone of the harmonic should be heard. A harmonic provides a subtle way to close a song or accent a note within a melody. Like some of the preceding techniques, harmonics may take some time to master.

Triplets

Triplets allow you to squeeze the sound of three notes between two picking actions. To sound a triplet, immediately after striking a string, hammer your ring finger on a fret, bringing the middle and index fingers down in rapid succession on the succeeding frets toward the bridge. This technique works equally well in reverse order. The only difference is that the index, middle, and ring fingers are already on their respective frets and they are pulled off of the finger board in the reverse order that they were hammered on. That is, first the index, then the middle, and then the ring finger.

Accompanying Other Instruments

Tuning the dulcimer to accompany another instrument is quite simple. First the dulcimer player must determine the proper mode in which to play a song. After the proper mode is determined, ask the person who is accompanying you in what key he will be playing. Tell him to sound the note named by that key. Tune the open bass string on the dulcimer to the note named by that key and then tune the remainder of the strings from the bass string to the proper mode for the song to be played.

For example, if you wish to accompany another instrument on a song you know sounds best played on the dulcimer in the Ionian mode, ask the person who is accompanying you in what key he will be playing the song. He might tell you the key of C. Ask him to sound a C, the note named by the key in which he is playing. Tune your open bass string on the dulcimer to this C, and then tune the remainder of the strings from the bass string to the Ionian tuning. This would mean the strings would be tuned to G, G, C in this instance.

Always remember when accompanying another instrument that the dulcimer is diatonically fretted; that is, it can be tuned to only one key in one mode at a time. This is in contrast with most other stringed instruments which are chromatically fretted, meaning that they have all of the possible notes of all keys on their finger boards.

The Cadwell's of Kentucky, circa 1930

Translating Printed Music

Translating printed music for use on the dulcimer can be helpful if you would like to learn a particular song. There are two sets of charts provided here, one for translating music to the Ionian mode, the other for translating music to the Aeolian mode.

To use the charts, decide to which mode you would like to translate a song. Most songs will sound better in the Ionian or major mode rather than in the Aeolian or minor mode. After your dulcimer is tuned to the proper mode, look at the key signature, the number of sharps or flats, of the song that you are going to translate. Then, within the group of charts for either the Ionian or the Aeolian mode, find the chart with the same key signature as the song you wish to translate. After you have found the proper chart, look at the notes in the song you wish to translate and compare them with the notes in the chart. This will tell you which frets on the melody string the notes in the song represent.

Songs with the following key signatures can be translated to the Ionian mode with this group of charts. The numbers below the notes are the frets on melody string these notes represent.

Songs with the following key signatures can be translated to the Aeolian mode with this group of charts. The numbers below the notes are the frets on the melody string these notes represent.

Key of C Major

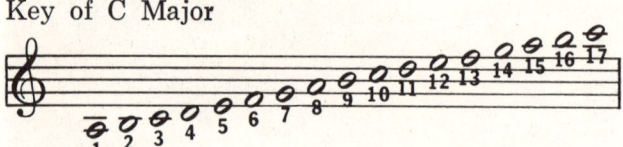

Key of A Minor

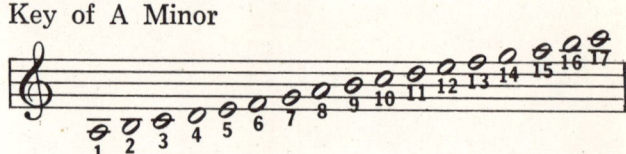

Key of G Major

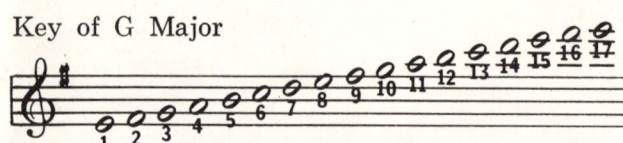

Key of E Minor

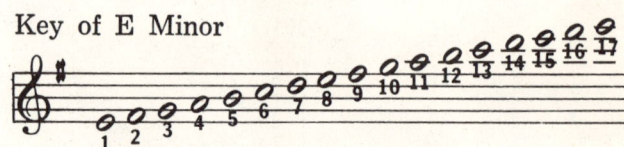

Key of D Major

Key of B Minor

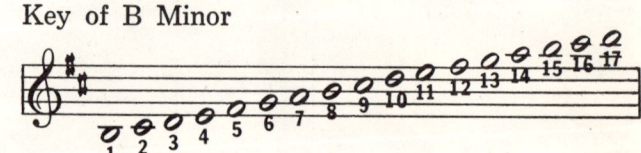

Key of A Major

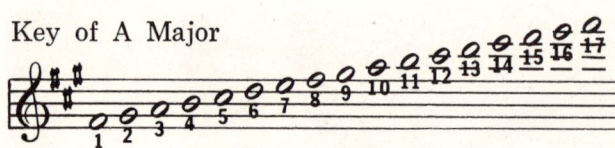

Key of F# Minor

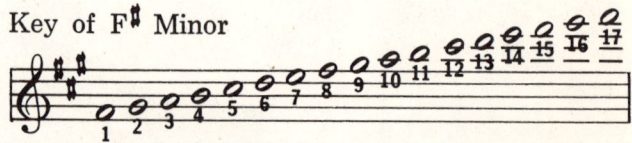

Key of E Major

Key of C# Minor

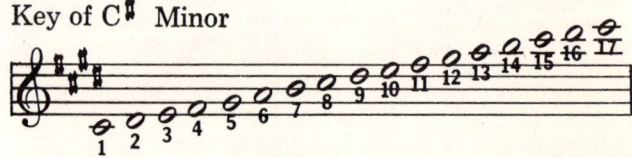

Unidentified group of musicians, circa 1930

For instance, to translate the following melody to the Ionian mode:

The dulcimer is first tuned to the Ionian mode. You then look at the key signature of the song. It contains one sharp. Within the group of charts for translating music to the Ionian mode, find the chart for translating a song with one sharp. Then compare the notes in the song with the notes in that chart to see which frets on the melody string the notes in the song represent.

3 3 1   3 4 3

The numbers below the notes indicate which frets should be depressed on the melody string.

91

APPENDIX

Buying a Dulcimer

Nothing is more futile than attempting to play on an improperly crafted instrument. If you follow the simple guidelines in this chapter when choosing your dulcimer, the chances are that it will serve your needs well.

However, if the idea of building your own dulcimer sounds enticing, there is a list of books on dulcimer construction along with sources for obtaining precut dulcimer wood at the end of this book. Unless you are an experienced woodworker or have some knowledge of musical instrument construction, building a dulcimer may prove to be a difficult task.

Most dulcimers have three or four strings. The only difference between them is that a four string dulcimer has a double melody string fretted as one string, while a three string dulcimer has a single melody string. Although a greater or lesser number of strings might be suited for particular playing purposes, three or four strings is the most practical number for a wide range of playing.

A fine dulcimer body utilizes well-seasoned solid wood cut approximately one eighth of an inch thick to achieve maximum resonance. The body's back and sides should be made of hardwood, while the sounding board should be comprised of softwood, preferably quarter sawn. Hardwood is used for the back and sides, since it deflects sound better than softwood. Softwood is used for the sounding board, since it is more resonant than hardwood and better amplifies the string's vibrations.

Aside from the wood used, there are subtle design differences that make a dulcimer better suited for particular playing styles or for playing in general. For instance, an instrument having fewer than fifteen frets will greatly limit your song repertoire, since high notes will be lacking. Also, the length of the frets determines the versatility of a dulcimer. Some instruments have frets that extend across the entire finger board, while others have frets under only the first string. Although many old dulcimers have short frets, this makes it impossible to use any progressive playing techniques, since only the first string can be fretted.

The frets should be properly positioned on the finger board. They can be tested by sounding each fret. If any of the intervals between the notes don't sound correct, chances are that some or all of the frets are improperly positioned. Also, if any of the frets buzz, it could mean that the finger board is warped and will need to be replaced.

Tuning pegs are critical parts of the instrument. Two types of pegs are commonly used, mechanical and wooden. Many wooden pegs are improperly fitted. Make certain the peg holes follow the same taper as the pegs, or the pegs won't hold the strings in tune. If a dulcimer has mechanical pegs, they should be checked; particularly if they are lower quality ungeared pegs. Mechanical pegs should turn smoothly and easily, so that they can be adjusted without difficulty.

Some dulcimers even have fine tuners incorporated in them for subtle string adjustments. There are two types of fine tuners, standard violin fine tuners, or sliding blocks of wood on an elevated plane between the bridge and the hitch pins. Though not necessary, fine tuners aid in bringing the strings to pitch more readily than the main tuning mechanisms.

Several details determine how easily an instrument can be played. For instance, if the fret board extends several inches below the bridge, your hand can be supported there as you strum the strings. Playing in a progressive style is easier if the height of the bridge is adjustable, since this permits the string action to be adjusted to the lowest possible height without the strings rattling on the frets.

Many features affect an instrument's tone. Scallops cut in the base of the sounding board or a hollow fret board enables the sounding board to resonate more freely, emitting a louder tone. The depth of the dulcimer's body also determines its bass response. The greater the body's depth, the more pronounced its bass response. Although basically an aesthetic point, all of the glue joints should be examined to see if they are securely fastened. The sides of the body should be checked for any hairline cracks which sometimes result when the sides are bent.

Dulcimer Repairs

The tone of a well-made dulcimer actually improves with age and wear, since its glue joints acquire added flexibility, permitting the sounding board to resonate more freely. However, it is quite possible that your instrument might need a few minor repairs for a variety of reasons. One of the greatest enemies of all wooden instruments is subjection to extremes in humidity. Therefore, never store your instrument in a damp or very dry location. A case is also a good investment, even if it is just a padded quilt with a draw string, since it will help to protect your dulcimer from the weather and from damage. If you are not going to play for several days, loosen your dulcimer's strings. They have a tendency to stretch out unevenly under tension, resulting in improper tonality. If the strings are replaced every several months, they will sound much more responsive.

Although doing any major repair work on your dulcimer is quite risky unless you know something about stringed instrument construction, the following explanations cover minor repairs that can be made quite easily with a minimum of tools.

Wooden tuning pegs expand or contract when the humidity changes. This may cause the pegs to stick or slip. Several substances, such as violin rosin, which can be obtained from a local music store, or ordinary blackboard chalk can be rubbed on the pegs to help them function more efficiently. If neither of these substances works suitably, a repair person should make the adjustment, since it requires specialized tools. Remember, wooden pegs are individually tapered and should always remain in their original holes.

The string action, the height of the strings above the frets, may need resetting. The higher the action, the more force that must be applied to fret the strings. However, if the action is too low, the strings may vibrate on the frets when they are strummed vigorously causing an annoying buzzing sound. The main regulator of the string action is the height of the string notches in the bridge. To see if the action is properly adjusted, make the following check. Push down each string at the second fret. The clearance over the third fret should not be less than one thirty-second of an inch to avoid buzzing. If the action is too high, deepen the notches in the bridge. The string notches in the bridge should be lower on the side facing the hitch pins or the strings will vibrate in the notches. Also, the notch for the bass string should not be as deep as it is for the other strings, since the bass string is larger in diameter. If the string notches in the bridge are too low, a wedge can usually be placed under each end of the bridge to prop it up.

There are several other possible reasons why the strings might buzz. One cause could be a loose fret. This can be remedied by removing the offending fret with a pair of pliers, placing some glue in the empty fret slot, and then hammering the fret into its slot. If the frets are protruding from the top of the finger board unevenly, this may also cause the strings to buzz. This problem can be alleviated by sanding down the frets until they are level with a piece of grade 440 sandpaper glued to a flat piece of wood. When the humidity is low, frets have a tendency to stick out from the sides of the finger board which may make fretting the strings painful. These protrusions can be leveled off the same way as the frets were leveled off on the top of the finger board.

Humidity changes or rough handling may cause small cracks in an instrument's body. These cracks can be fixed quite simply by placing a small amount of white or hide glue on the crack and then rubbing it in with a sharp object. The crack is then clamped shut, and the excess glue is sanded off after it has dried.

Repairs of a greater magnitude than these are best left to a competent repair person. However, if you wish to disassemble a dulcimer yourself, you can do it in various ways, depending on the type of glue with which it was constructed. Two types of glue are commonly used, white and hide glue. When dry, white glue is almost clear, while hide glue has an amber to brownish tint. A white glue joint can be separated by placing a heat lamp near the joint which you wish to disassemble, since heat makes the glue malleable. A hide glue joint can be separated by cutting the joint with a hot knife. Never use epoxy glue for repairs if you ever wish to disassemble the instrument again.

If your instrument might need refinishing, it can be done in several ways, depending with what it has already been coated. Lacquer or varnish usually has a shiny appearance and will wear with time. Either of these coatings can be removed with a commercial finish remover, leaving the wood ready to be sanded and refinished. A variety of wood oils, such as tung or linseed oil, can be used to refinish an instrument. Although an oil finish can't be readily removed, it can be refurbished occasionally by rubbing in a little more oil. To preserve a dulcimer's finish, wax the wood occasionally.

Dulcimer Makers List

This list of Appalachian dulcimer makers is provided for people who might like to purchase a dulcimer. Most of these craftsmen will sell their instruments by mail. This listing does not constitute a personal recommendation by myself for the quality or the service of these craftsmen. If there are any other dulcimer makers who would like to be mentioned in a revised edition of this book, please contact me. If someone might be interested in purchasing a hammered dulcimer, banjo, guitar, mandolin, or a reproduction of an historical instrument, I also make these instruments, besides making Appalachian dulcimers.

Adams, Paul, C/O Sea Way Marina, Box 3434, 7012 N. Galena Rd., Peoria, Ill. 61614
Alpine Dulcimer Co., Box 566, Boulder, Col. 80302
Antes, Scott, Route 1, Box 130, Hanover, Indiana 47243
Apollonio, Nick, Box 221 Main St., Rockport, Me. 04856
Appalachian Dulcimer Corp., 232 W. Frederick St., Staunton, Va. 24401
Autorino, Michael, Rt. 2, W. Searsville Rd., Montgomery, N. Y. 12549
Bailey, John, Warfleet Creek, Dartmouth, Devon, England
Beall, Jerrold, Rt. 1, Swans Rd., Newark, Ohio 43055
Behlen, Stinson, 1010 South 14th St., Slaton, Texas 79364
Bishop, Geoffrey, 295 N. Hartz, Danville, Cal. 94526
Bond, Frank, 13 Lancaster Road, London, N. 11, England
Brewer, George F., 300 Islington Rd., Auburndale, Mass. 02166
Brown, Edwin, 33242 Redwood Blvd., Avon Lake, Ohio 44012
Bryan, Bob, 401 Roxanne Drive, Raleigh, N. C. 27603
Capritaurus Dulcimers, P. O. Box 153, Felton, Cal. 95018
Carol, Bonnie, Wallstreet, Salina Star Route, Boulder, Colo. 80302
Caskey, Tom, Route 1, Box 188A, Lawton, Michigan 49065
Childs, Courtney, 789 Maher Rd., Watsonville, Cal. 95076
Christian, Bob, 2 Downrew Cottage, Bishops Tawton, North Devon, England
Clifford, Roger, R.F.D. 2, Box 132, Bangor, Maine 04401
Daniellson, Jim, 655 E. 32nd Ave., Eugene, Oregon 97405
Davis, Bill, Gatlinburg, Tenn. 37738
Diamond Dulcimers, 2317 Briggs Road, Silver Springs, Md. 20906
Dickson, Reverend Gordon, Montauk Highway, E. Moriches, N. Y. 11940
Dixon, Judge, Whitesburg, Kentucky 41858
Dixon, Robert, 224 East Elm St., East Rochester, N.Y. 14445
Dorogi, Dennis, Ellicott Rd., Brockton, N. Y. 14716
Doty, Dan, 3773 Wychemere, Memphis, Tenn. 38128
Dulcimer Shop, The, P. O. Box 110, Mountain View, Arkansas 72560
Dulcimer Shoppe, The, 620 E. Broadway, Forrest City, Ark. 72335
Dulcimer Works, The, 1723 W. Washington Blvd., Venice, Cal. 90291
Elder Workshop, Lyn, Industrial Center Bldg. Annex, Gate 5 Rd., Sausalito, Cal. 94965
Ellis, W. B., The Coach House, Dilwyn, Herefordshire, England
English, Larry, Hwy. 4, P.O. Box 615, Arnold, Cal. 95223
Field, Dave, 237 Lexington Ave., Pitman, N. J. 08071
Frederick, Peach, Mystic Hills, Rt. 69, Wintersport, Maine 04496
Freeman, Morris, P. O. Box 393, Paradise, Cal. 95969
Glenn, Clifford and Leonard, Rt. 2, Banner Elk, N. C. 28604
Gonzales, Joseph, 529 Indian Hill Blvd., Claremont, Cal. 91711
Gotzmer Stringed Instruments, Route 2, Box 2286A, La Plata, Md. 20646
Green River Dulcimers, Box 659, Elkhorn, Ky. 42733
Hall, Jack, Route 3, Box 170, Whitesburg, Kentucky 41858
Harmon, Bob, Blowing Rock, N. C. 28605
Harris, Allan, 3 Clark St., Eastport, Maine 04631
Here Inc., 410 Cedar Ave., Minneapolis, Minn. 55404
Hicks, Stanley, Sugar Grove, N. C. 28679
Hines, Chet, 9760 E. Hasket Lane, Dayton, Ohio 45424
Hughes, Virgil, 8665 W. 13th Ave., Denver, Col. 80215
Johnson, M., 2 Bassett Place, Falmouth, Cornwall, England
Kardos, Andrew R., 6605 So. 85th St., Ralston, Nebr. 68127
Kearney, Tam, 199 Erskine Ave., Toronto, Canada
Kelischek, George, Brasstown, N. C. 28902
Kimball, Dean, R. R. 1, Box 127A, Yellow Springs, Ohio 45387
Kinsolving, Pitt, 7 Silk St., Norwalk, Conn. 06850
Lamoreaux, Cal, R.R. 1, Shelbyville, Mich. 49344
Ledford, Homer, 125 Sunset Heights, Winchester, Kentucky 40391
Litster, Gordon, 1857 Feltham Rd., Victoria, Canada
Live Wood, P. O. Box 50, Fall Creek, Oregon 97438
Luke Dulcimers, 22 Crandol Drive, Tabb, Virginia 23602
Magic Mountain Workshop, Box 614, Mill Valley, Cal. 94941
Manley, Dick, Route 129, Croton-On-Hudson, N.Y. 10620
Martin, Edsel, Box 367, Swannannoa, N. C. 28778
Martindale, Howard, Dean Rd., Hudson Falls, N.Y. 12839
Maxwell, John, 545 East 20th St., Cookeville, Tenn. 38501
Meades, Jim, Ripley Rd., Spencer, W. Va. 25276
Medearis, Douglas, Box 273, Winnebago, Illinois 61088
Melton, Raymond, Rt. 1, Box 211, Woodlawn, Va. 24381
Mize, Robert, Route 2, Blountville, Tenn. 37617
Montague, Fred, 16 Patriot Rd., Tewksbury, Mass. 01876
Muelrath, Dave, General Delivery, Forest Glen, Trinity County, Cal. 26030
Murphy, Michael, Mills Road, R. R. 3, St. Clairsville, Ohio 43950
Musical Traditions, 2375 Edgewater Terrace, Los Angeles, Cal. 90039
Nicholas, General Custor and Sons, Rt. 3, Carrollton, Ohio 44615
Peck, Elizabeth, 932 Hilltop Mobile Home Ct., Ashville, N. C. 28803
Perlman, Alan, Windham R. F. D., West Townsend, Vt. 05359
Pickow, George, 7A Locust Ave., Port Washington, N. Y. 11050
Presnell, Edd, Box 235, Banner Elk, N. C. 28604

Proffitt, Frank, Jr., Rt. 2, Todd, N. C. 28684
Pyle, Paul, 414 Campbell St., Tullahoma, Tenn. 37388
Ranney, Bob, P.O. Box 4623 GS, Springfield, Missouri 65804
Reisler, Paul, Rt. 1, Box 99, Keyser, W. Va. 26726
Rizetta String Instruments, 4616 So. 1st St., Arlington, Va. 22204
Romine, Don, 4724 N. W. 59th St., Oklahoma City, Oklahoma 73122
Round, Donald, 6470 Eighth Ave., Grandville, Michigan 49418
Sams, J. D., Sardis Rd., Euka, N. C.
Schilling, Jean and Lee, P. O. Box No. 8, Cosby, Tenn. 37722
Sears, Lynn, Star Route 1, Box 15A, Covelo, Cal. 95428
Seedpod, Galiano Island, British Columbia, Canada
Shuttleworth, Don, R. R. No. 3, Warren, Indiana 46792
Spence, Bill, R. D. 1, Wormer Road, Voorheesville, N. Y. 12186
Stanley, Pete, 15 Torriano Avenue, London, NW5 2SN, England
Sunhearth, R. D. 1, Box 74, Roaring Springs, Pa. 16673
Tignor, John, Route 7, Frankfort, Ky. 40601
Torstenson, Ray, 301 So. Plymouth Rd., Huntsville, Ala. 35811
Tugel, Ake, 266 Sea Cliff Ave., Sea Cliff, N. Y. 11579
Vogel, Robert, 2835 Alba Rd., Ben Lomond, Cal. 95005
Voorhees, Clark, Weston, Vermont 05161
Ward, N. T., Jr., Vilas, N. C. 28692
Wasel, Bill, 451 11th Ave., S., St. Petersburg, Fl. 33731
Wilson, Max, R. R. 3, Paoli, Indiana 47454
Wurtz, Howard P., 2503 Medcliff Rd., Santa Barbara, Cal. 93105
Young, Henry, 153 W. Warren, Germantown, Ohio 45327
Young, Jerry, R. F. D. 1, Box 46A, Robbinston, Maine 04671

Sources for Buying Dulcimer Wood

The following companies and individuals, including myself, sell precut dulcimer wood by mail. This listing does not constitute a personal recommendation for the quality of the wood or the service of these companies or individuals.

Craftsman Wood Service, 2727 South Mary St., Chicago, Illinois 60608
Green River Dulcimers, Elkhorn, Ky. 42733
Guitar Center, Box 15444, Tulsa, Oklahoma 74115
Gurian Guitars, Canal St., Hinsdale, New Hampshire 03451
Joseph F. Wallo, 1319 F St. Northwest, Washington, D.C. 20004
Metropolitan Music Co., 222 Park Ave. South, N. Y., N. Y. 10003
Michael Murphy, Mills Road, R. R. 3, St. Clairsville, Ohio 43950
Vitali Import Co., 5944-48 Atlantic Blvd., Maywood, Cal. 90270

Other Dulcimer Instruction Books

Appalachian Dulcimer, The, A. W. Jeffreys, Staunton, Virginia 24401. 1958
Brethren, We Have Met, Lynn McSpadden, The Dulcimer Shop, P. O. Box 110, Mountain View, Arkansas 72560. 1970
Dulcimer Book, The, Jean Ritchie, Oak Publications, N. Y. 1963
Dulcimer Instruction Book, Stinson R. Behlen, Southern Highlands Dulcimers, Slaton, Texas 79364
Dulcimer Player's Bible, The, Phillip Mason, R.F.D. 2, Box 132, Bangor, Maine 04401. 1975
Four and Twenty Songs for the Mountain Dulcimer, Lynn McSpadden, The Dulcimer Shop, P.O. Box 110, Mountain View, Arkansas 72560. 1970
Fun With the Dulcimer, Virgil Hughes, Mel Bay Publications, Kirkwood, Missouri
How to Play the Dulcimer, Margaret Winters, Boston Music Co., Boston, Mass. 1953
How to Play the Dulcimer, A Manual for Beginners, H. S. Evans, Lynchburg, Virginia 24505. 1969
How to Play the Dulcimer Today, David Kay, Chas Hasen Books, N. Y. 1974
How to Tune and Play the Dulcimer, Paul Pyle Studios, Tullahoma, Tenn. 37388
In Search of the Wild Dulcimer, Robert Force and Albert D' Ossche, Vintage Books, N. Y. 1974
Life Is Like a Mountain Dulcimer, Neal Hellman and Sally Holden, Ludlow Music Corp., N. Y. 1974
Moods of the Dulcimer (two volumes), Mel Bay Publications, Kirkwood, Missouri. 1975
Musicks Delite on the Dulcimer, Roger Nicholson, Scratchwood Music, London. 1974
Nonesuch for Dulcimer, Roger Nicholson, Scratchwood Music, London. 1972
Play the Dulcimer by Ear and Other Easy Ways, Sue and Len MacEachron, Here Inc., Box 341, Minneapolis, Minnesota 55440. 1970
Playing Lead Dulcimer, Richard Wilkie, 3 Cities Press, 192 Mount Hope Drive, Albany, N. Y. 12202. 1974
Plucked Dulcimer and How to Play It, The, John F. Putnam, 1905 Hopefield Road, Silver Springs, Maryland 20904. 1961

Construction Books

Constructing the Mountain Dulcimer, Dean Kimball, McKay, N. Y. 1974
Dulcimer Book, The, John Pearse, English Song and Dance Society, London. 1970
Dulcimer People, The, Jean Ritchie, Oak Publications, N. Y. 1975
How to Make and Play the Dulcimer, Chet Hines, Stackpole Books, Harrisburg, Pa. 1974
Making an Appalachian Dulcimer, John Baily, English Song and Dance Society, London 1966
Mountain Dulcimer, The — How to Make It and Play It, Howard W. Mitchell, Folk Legacy Records, Sharon, Connecticut. 1966.
To Build a Dulcimer, Paul Pyle Studios, 414 Campbell Ave., Tullahoma, Tenn. 37388

Bibliography

Adler, Tom "How to Make an Appalachian Dulcimer, or, What to Do With Your Spare Time and Money." *Autoharp,* no. 30, Oct. 20, 1967. Reprinted in *Folknik,* vol. 4, no. 5, Sept., 1968

Apel, Willi *Harvard Dictionary of Music,* second edition. Harvard University Press, 1969. See, "Dulcimer."

Bell, Corydon "The Fair at Gatlinburg." *Ford Times,* July, 1950

Bell, Red "Build a Dulcimer." *Stray Notes,* vol. 1, no. 6, Nov., 1965

Bishop, Elinor Hopper "Newcomer at Home in the Center of the Area Musical Activity." *Foothill Life,* Monrovia, Cal., May 7, 1966

Boette, Marie *Singa Hipsy Doodle and Other Folk Songs of West Virginia,* The Junior League of Parkersburg, W. Va., 1971, p. XV

Brewer, Mary T. "A Golden Memory." *Mountain Life and Work,* vol. XL, no. 2, Berea, Ky., Summer, 1964

Brunvard, Jan Herold *The Study of American Folklore.* Norton, 1967

Bryan, Charles Faulkner "American Folk Instruments: The Appalachian Dulcimer." *Tenn. Folklore Soc. Bulletin,* vol. 18, no. 1, Mar., 1952. Also, June, 1952, and Sept., 1952

"The Appalachian Dulcimer Enigma." *Tenn. Folklore Soc. Bulletin,* vol. 20, no. 4, Dec., 1954

Burch, Gladys "Young Lady With a Dulcimer." *American Girl,* Aug., 1951

Burcham, Terry W. "Joe Gambill Dulcimer to Opryland." *Huntsville Assn. of Folk Musicians Newsletter,* no. 46, June 20, 1972

"Mountain Dulcimer." *Huntsville Assn. of Folk Musicians Newsletter,* no. 49, Sept. 20, 1972

Burrison, John "Biography of a Folk Singer." *Folkways Monthly,* Jan., 1963

Campbell, John C. *The Southern Highlander and His Homeland.* Russell Sage Foundation, N. Y., 1921, pp. 143-4

Clarke, Kenneth and Mary *A Concise Dictionary of Folklore.* Ky. Folklore Series, no. 1, by *Ky. Folklore Record,* W. Ky. State College, Bowling Green, Ky., 1965

Cobb, Ann "Dulcimer Over the Fireboard." *Literary Digest,* vol. 62, Sept. 27, 1919, p. 33

Combs, Jack "The Folk Singers of the Kentucky Highlands . . . A Trip to Hindman." *Spectrum,* vol. 1, no. 2, Spring, 1963

Combs, Josiah H. "The Highlander's Music." *Kentucky Folklore Record,* vol. 5, no. 4, Oct.-Dec., 1959; first published in *Vient de Paraitre,* Paris 1926. Unused chapter of Dr. Combs' doctoral thesis, Sorbonne, 1925. Later included in the publication of the thesis as *Folk Songs of the Southern United States,* American Folklore Society, Texas, 1967

Creighton, Mildred Davidson "Jethro Amburgy: Dulcimer Maker." *Appalachian South,* vol. 1, no. 1, Summer, 1965

Davidson, Luckett "Learning Dulcimer is Kid Stuff . . ." *The Louisville Times,* Mar. 3, 1966, p. A34

Downs, Floyd and Mrs. Discussion under "Folklore," in the *Association for Childhood Education International Program,* 1950 Study Conference, Ashville, N. C., p. 32. Reprinted from *Souvenir Program, Craftsman's Fair of the Southern Highland,* 1949

Drager, Hans-Heinz "Die Musik in Geschichte und Gegenwart." vol. 5, 1956, cols. 1210-1211

Eaton, Allen W. *Handicrafts of the Southern Highlands.* Russell Sage Foundation, N. Y., 1937, pp. 199-204

English Folk Dance and Song Society Journal, vol. 2, 1935, "A Norwegian Player on the Langeleik."

Fetterman, John "Tennessee Hill Country Dulcimer Builder." *Tennessean Magazine,* May 30, 1954

Foxfire, vol. 8, no. 3, Fall, 1974, "Robert Mize, Dulcimer Maker."

Gilfallan, Merrill C. "Dulcimers." *The Wonderful World of Ohio,* vol. 30, no. 1, Jan., 1966 (Dulcimer collection of Ann Grimes)

Glassie, Henry *Pattern of the Material Folk Culture in the Eastern U. S.* Philadelphia, 1968

Glenn, Leonard "The Plucked Dulcimer of the Southern Appalachians." *Folkways Monthly,* vol. 1, no. 2, Jan., 1963

Griffin, Gerald "Transition in the Mountains." *The Courier-Journal Magazine,* Louisville, Ky., May 25, 1952

Guthrie, A. B., Jr. "Kentucky." *Holiday* magazine, Fifth Anniversary Issue

Haines, Aubrey B. "The John Jacob Niles Story." *Mature Years,* March-May, 1972, Cokesbury Press, Nashville, Tenn.

Hamilton, Judith "The Mountain Dulcimer." *The Ozarks Mountaineer,* vol. 19, no. 2, Mar., 1971

Hammer, Philip L. "If You Like Mountain Music . . ." *Science and Mechanics,* vol. 35, no. 1, Jan., 1964

Hansen, Barbara "Sweet Dulcimer Sounds Rent Air in Southland." *Los Angeles Herald & Express,* April 27, 1961, p. D-2

Hart, Tim "The Appalachian Dulcimer." *Club Folk,* vol. 1, no. 5, July-Aug., 1968

Hastings, S. E., Jr. "Construction Techniques in an Old Appalachian Mountain Dulcimer." *Journal of American Folklore,* vol. 83, no. 330, Oct.-Dec., 1970

Herndon, Doris Arlene *"The Appalachian Dulcimer, Its History and Origin."* unpublished M. A. thesis, University of North Dakota, 1967

Hickerson, Joseph C. *A Bibliography of Hammered and Plucked (Appalachian or Mountain) Dulcimers and Related Instruments,* Library of Congress, Music Division, Archive of Folk Song, Washington, D. C. 20540, Jan., 1973. Rev. from an earlier edition published in the *Journal of the Folklore Society of Greater Washington,* vol. 3, nos. 1-2, Summer, 1972

Hipkins, A. J. "Dulcimer." *Grove's Dictionary of Music and Musicians,* fifth edition. Ed. by Eric Blom. London; Macmillan & Co. Ltd., vol. 5, pp. 799-800, 1954

Horwitz, Elinor Lander *Mountain People, Mountain Crafts.* J. B. Lippincott Co., Philadelphia, N. Y., 1974, pp. 20-34

Hoskins, R. Springer "Making Dulcimers is More Than a Hobby." (Story about A. L. Greynolds). *The Harlan Daily Enterprise,* Harlan, Ky., April 7, 1966, p. 4

Hughes, Jean "Your Pick of Appalachian Dulcimers." *Popular Science Magazine,* Dec., 1973

Irish Independent, Nov. 8, 1952, Dublin, Eire, "Of Ballads, Songs and Snatches . . ." p. 5, signed with initials I. M.

Jamison, Gladys V. "They Came Singing." *Mountain Life and Work,* vol. XXXIX, no. 2, Summer, 1963

Jeffreys, A. W. "Dulcimer Papers History." Papers presented before the Virginia Folklore Society and the Forum Club of Staunton, Virginia

Jong, J. L. de *"Mens en Melodie."* vol. 12, no. 6, 1957, pp. 174-176

Lawless, Ray M. *Folksingers and Folksongs in America.* Duell, Sloan and Pearce, N. Y., 1960. Rev. ed., 1965. Chapter 9, "Folk Music Instruments."

Leach, Maria *Dictionary of Folklore Mythology and Legend.* Funk & Wagnalls Co., N. Y., 1949. See, "Dulcimer."

McGill, Josephine "The Kentucky Mountain Dulcimer." *The Musician,* vol. 22, no. 1, Jan., 1917, p. 21

Marais, Joseph and Miranda *World Folk Songs.* Ballantine Books, New York, 1964, pp. 127-207

Marcuse, Sibyl *Musical Instruments: A Comprehensive Dictionary.* Doubleday & Co., Garden City, N. Y., 1964. See, "Appalachian Dulcimer," "Epinette," "Humle," "Hummel," "Langeleik," "Scheitholt"

Mellon, Robert "Mountain Maestro of Hudson Falls." *Adirondack Life,* vol. 3, no. 1, Winter, 1972

Mercer, Henry C. "The Zithers of the Pennsylvania Germans." *A Collection of Papers Read Before the Bucks County Historical Society,* vol. 5, 1926

Meyer, Carolyn "Handmade in America: The Delightful Mountain Dulcimer." *McCalls* magazine, vol. 98, no. 8, May, 1971

Miles, E. B. "Dulcimore." *Harpers Magazine,* vol. 119, Nov., 1909, pp. 949-956

Mize, Robert "Dulcimers." *Foxfire* magazine, vol. 3, no. 1, Spring, 1969

Mugwumps Instrument Herald, vol. 1, no. 2, 1972, pp. 8-9

Muller, Barbara *Dulcimer Sound and Picture Guide.* Hobbs Productions, Edgewater, Florida

Nicholson, Roger A. "The Appalachian Dulcimer." *Spin* magazine, Wallasey, Cheshire, England, vol. 5, no. 6, 1968; *Folknik,* San Francisco Folk Music Club Newsletter, vol. 4, no. 5, Sept., 1968

Norlind, Tobias *Systematik der Saiteninstrumente.* vol. 1, *Geschichte der Zither.* Musikhistorisches Museum, Stockholm, 1936. See, "Trapezzither," and "Hummel."

Niles, John Jacob "Deft Hands Carve the Dulcimer." *Courier-Journal Magazine,* Jan. 20, 1952

Odell, Scott "The Appalachian Dulcimer." *1968 Festival of American Folklife* program booklet, Washington, D. C., Smithsonian Institution
Arts in Virginia, vol. 12, no. 1, 1971, pp. 31-37

Panum, Hortense *Langelegen: Som Danst Folkeinstrument.* Lehmann & State, Copenhagen, 1917. Two volumes.
Stringed Instruments of the Middle Ages. Translated by Jeffrey Pulver. Wm. Reeves, London, 1939; reprinted by Greenwood Press, Westport, Conn., 1970, and Da Capo Press, N. Y., 1971. See, "The Scheitholt Family."

Pearson, Candace "My Kind of Music." *Daily Pilot,* Riverside, Cal., April 3, 1972

Pickow, George "Dulcimer Maker." *Scenic South,* Aug., 1955, p. 16

Pound, Louise *American Ballads and Songs*

Proffitt, Frank "Good Memories For Me." *Sing Out!* vol. 15, no. 5, Nov., 1965

Promenade magazine, vol. 1, no. 7, Oct., 1940: "Musical Instruments of the American Folk."

Putnam, John F. "The Plucked Dulcimer." *Mountain Life and Work,* vol. 34, no. 4, 1958
The Plucked Dulcimer of the Southern Mountains. Council of the Southern Mountains, Berea, Ky., 1957; rev. 1972

Ritchie, Jean *Singing Family of the Cumberlands.* Oxford U. Press, N. Y., 1955; reprinted by Oak Publications, N. Y., 1963

Roginski, Jerianne "Dulcimers — Who Sells Them." *Billboard,* Aug. 26, 1967

Russcol, Herb "Lonesome Ballits and Courtin' Songs." *Venture* magazine, July-Aug., 1969

Scarborough, Dorothy *A Song Catcher of the Southern Highlands.* New York, 1937, pp. 70-72.

Schecter, Martha *Dulcimer Tuning.* M. Schecter, Rm. 14, N-211, M.I.T., Cambridge, Mass., 1970

Seeger, Charles "The Appalachian Dulcimer." *Journal of American Folklore,* vol. 71, no. 279, Jan.-Mar., 1958

Seeger, Peter "Johnny Appleseed, Jr.," column in *Sing Out!* magazine, vol. 9, no. 1, N.Y., Summer, 1959

Sharp, Cecil *English Folk Songs of the Southern Highlands.* Oxford Press, London, 1953, pp. XXIII-XIX

Shoemaker, Henry W. *The Music and Musical Instruments of the Pennsylvania Mountaineers.* Times Tribune Co., Altoona, Pa., 1923

Smith, Ralph Lee "Some Pointers for Beginning Dulcimer Players." *Sing Out!,* vol. 20, no. 2, Nov.-Dec., 1970

Snortheim, Olaf "Der Langeleik in Norwegian." *Pro Musica: Blatter fur Musik von Volk zu Volk,* no. 1, Jan.-Feb., 1953

Sorosi, Balint *Die Volksmusikinstrumente Ungarns.* VEB Deutscher Verlag fur Musik, Serie I, Band I, Leipzig, 1968

Stambler, Irwin, and Grelun Landon *Encyclopedia of Folk, Country and Western Music.* St. Martins Press, N. Y., 1969. See, "Appalachian Dulcimer." Also, profiles of dulcimer players Paul Clayton, John Jacob Niles, Frank Proffitt, Jean Ritchie and Andrew Rowen Summers.

Steffens, Arlene "The Southern Highland Dulcimer and Its Craftsman." *Music Clubs Magazine,* vol. 49, no. 3, 1970

Stephens, Rockwell "The Mountain Dulcimer." *Vermont Life,* vol. 24, no. 1, Autumn, 1969

Stradner, Fritz "Eine Alte Scheitholz-Zither." *Osterreichische Musikzeitschrift,* vol. 21, no. 9, Sept., 1966
"Vom Scheithol zur Kratz-Zither: Ein Beitrag zur Entwicklungsgeschechte der Zither." *Jahrbuch des Osterreishischen Volksliedwerkes,* vol. 18, 1969

Street, Julia Montgomery "Mountain Dulcimer." *North Carolina Folklore,* vol. 14, no. 2, Nov., 1966

Strickland, Sandy "Mastered Mountain Skill of Whittling." (Elizabeth Peck) *Jacksonville Journal,* Jan. 17 1972

Sturgill, Virgil L. "The History of the Dulcimer." *Washington Folk Strums,* no. 1, April 1, 1964; no. 2, May 1, 1964

Talley, Rhea "Ambassador From Kentucky." *Courier-Journal Magazine,* Louisville, Ky.

Taylor, Vernon H. "From Fact to Fancy in Dulcimer Discoveries." *Tennessee Folklore Society Bulletin,* vol. 23, no. 4, Dec., 1957

Thomas, David "A Little Bit About the Appalachian Dulcimer." *Milwaukee Folk,* vol. 1, no. 3, 1972

Thomas, Jean, and Joseph A. Leeder *The Singin' Gatherin'; Tunes From the Southern Appalachians.* Silver Burdett Co., N. Y., 1939. See, "Mountain Instruments and Their Usage." pp. 54-57

Tucker, George H. "A Love Ballad Needs a Dulcimore..." Norfolk *Virginia-Pilot,* June 22, 1969

Walin, Stig *Die Schwedische Hummel: Eine Instrumentenkindliche Untersuchung.* Nordiska Museet, Stockholm, 1952

Warner, Frank *Folk Songs and Ballads of the Eastern Seaboard: From a Collector's Notebook.* A lecture at Wesleyan College, Macon, Ga. Southern Press, Inc., 1963

West Virginia Hillbilly, June 15, 1974, "What We Have Learned About the Dulcimer." pp. 6-7

Wilcox, Lee "You Can Make Sweet Music on the Appalachian Dulcimer."*House Beautiful,* vol. 104, no. 10, Oct., 1962

Wilhelm, Eugene J., Jr., and R. G. Carlson "Behind the Blue Ridge Song." *Mountain Life and Work,* vol. XLV, no. 4, April, 1969

Woehl, Waldemer *Kurze Spielanweisung fur das Scheitholz,* Hausmusikverlag Soyen, Waldbockelheim, ub Bad Kreuznach, 1951

Die neuen Saiteninstrumente: Scheitholz und Psalterium (stapled mimeographed leaflets describing the instruments for sale), same address, 1960

Discography

The dulcimer discography below includes not only recent recordings, but also early recordings, many of which are currently unavailable. These early recordings are included, since they are continually being reissued.

Individual Performers, Families, Groups

Andersen, Ila *Ila*. With dulcimer. Order from Andersens, 7799 South Turkey Creek Rd., Morrison, Colorado 80465

Arkansaw Travellers *Arkansaw Travellers*. Various artists with dulcimer. ALP, 109
  Arkansaw Travellers Folk Theatre. With dulcimer. Arkansaw Traveller Theatre, Hardy, Arkansas

Armstrong, George and Gerry *Simple Gifts*. Dulcimer and guitar. Folkways, FA 2335. 1961

Beers, Evelyne and Bob *Evelyne and Bob Beers*. With dulcimer. Biograph, 12045
  Gentleness in Living. Philo, 1010
  Seasons of Peace. Biograph, 12033
  Walkie in the Parlor. Folkways, 2376

Bennett, Marjorie *Sing a Song of Childhood*. Dulcimer, autoharp, guitar, Irish harp. Judson Records, J-3028

Bergerfolk *Bergerfolk Sing for Joy*. Folkways, 32415
  Happy Landings. Folkways, 32416
  Sing of Sunshine and Rainbows. Folkways, 32417

Block, Allen and Smith, Ralph *Allen Block and Ralph Lee Smith*. Dulcimer, fiddle, guitar. Meadowlands Records, MS-1

Brand, Oscar *Courting's A Pleasure*. Electra, 122. 1957
  Jean Ritchie, Oscar Brand, and David Sear at Town Hall. Dulcimer, guitar, banjo. Folkways, FA 2428. 1959
  Oscar Brand and Jean Ritchie. Archive of Folk Music, FS 207

Brock, Louise and Dan *Kentucky Song Bag*. Lemco, LLP 702

Buckley, Bruce *Ohio Valley Ballads*. Guitar, dulcimer. Folkways, FA 2025

Burcham, Terry *Galax 73*. Tennvale, 002

Clayton, Paul *Cumberland Mountain Songs*. Dulcimer, guitar. Folkways, FA 1007. 1957
  Dulcimer Songs and Solos. Folkways, FA 2382

Coltman, Bob *Lonesome Robin*. Minstrel, JD 200

Critics Group *A Merry Progress to London*. Argo, ZDA 46

Davies, Bill and Jean. Recorded dulcimer selections for Tradition Records. No other information available.

Dildine Family *Dildine Family*. Front Hall, 103

Fairport Convention *Angel Delight*. A&M, 4319
  Full House. A&M, 4265

Farina, Richard and Mimi *Best of Richard and Mimi Farina*. Dulcimer, guitar, and other instruments. Vanguard, VSD 21/22
  Celebrations for a Grey Day. Dulcimer, guitar, autoharp. Vanguard, VRS 9174 (mono), and VSD 79174 (stereo). 1965
  Memories. Dulcimer, guitar, and other instruments. Vanguard, VSD 79263. 1968
  Reflections in a Crystal Wind. Dulcimer, guitar. Vanguard, VSD 79204. 1965
  Singer, Songwriter Project. Electra, EKS 7299

Gainer, Patrick *Folk Songs of the Alleghenies*. Folk Heritage Records, DB 2122-3

Greer, Mr. and Mrs. I. G. Recordings for Paramount Co., New York. No other information available. 1929

Grey, Sara *Sara Grey with Ed Trickett*. Folk Legacy, FSI 38

Grimes, Ann *Ohio State Ballads*. With dulcimer. Folkways, FH 5217. 1957

Hall, Kenny *Kenny Hall*. Dulcimer, mandolin, fiddle, guitar. Philo, 1008. 1975

Hart, Tim and Prior, Maddy. Recorded dulcimer selections for B&C Records and Tepee Records. No other information available

Ledford, Homer *How to Play the Dulcimer*. 45 rpm instruction record. Order from Ledfords, 125 Sunset Heights, Winchester, Ky. 40391
  The Ledford Family (Songs We Love to Sing and Play). Order from the Ledfords, same address as above. 1972

Library of Congress, Division of Music Recording.
  The following songs with dulcimer accompaniment are listed in the *Checklist of Recorded Songs in the English Language in the Archive of American Folk Music to July, 1940*.
  Sung with dulcimer accompaniment: 291 A, Run, Nigger, Run; 302 A1, Ground Hog; 302 A2, Turnip Greens; 302 B, Barbara Allen; 1342 B2, Little Brown Jug; 1540 A2, Henry of Knoxville; 1540 B, Barbara Allen; 1541 A, The Knoxville Girl; 2854 A1, George Collins; 2855 A1, Ground Hog; 3161 A1, Over the River Charlie; 3161 A3, Sally Brown.
  Dulcimer instrumentals: 1340 B1, Liza Jane; 1342 A3, Sourwood Mountain; 1342 B1, Turkey in the Straw; 1343 A5, Water Bound; 1343 B2, Arkansas Traveler; 1343 B3, Brown Eyes; 1343 B4, Liza Jane; 1347 A1, Turkey Buzzard; 1347 A2, Going Down the Road Feeling Bad; 1541 B2, Sourwood Mountain; 1541 B3, Old Granny Hare; 1553 A1, Buck Creek Girls; 1553 B1, Redwing; 1553 B3, The Wreck of Old 97; 3160 B1-3, Water Bound; 3160 B4, Turkey in the Straw; 3160 B5, Bonaparte's Retreat.

MacArthur, Margaret *On the Mountains High*. Dulcimer, guitar, harp, dobro, fiddle, banjo. Living Folk Records, LFR-100. 1971

Martin, Edsel *Edsel Martin Plays the Appalachian Dulcimer*. Vibrant Records

Mayhan, Judy *Folk Songs of Old Eire*. Tradition, 2075

Mitchell, Howie *Howie Mitchell*. With dulcimer. Folk Legacy Records, FSI 2. 1962
  The Mountain Dulcimer, How to Make It and Play It. Folk Legacy Records, FSI-29 (Record and booklet may be bought separately). 1966

Mitchell, Joni *Blue*. Reprise, 2038

Moser, Artus *North Carolina Mountain Folk Songs*. Folkways, 5331
  North Carolina Ballads. Dulcimer and guitar. Folkways, 2112. 1955

Muller, Eric and Koehler, Barbara. Dulcimer, banjo, guitar. Frailing Records.

Nicholson, Roger *Roger Nicholson*. With dulcimer. Trailer

Records, LER 3034
The Gentle Sound of the Dulcimer. Argo, 2DA 204
Niles, John Jacob *American Folk and Gambling Songs.* With dulcimer. RCA Camden, CAL-219
American Folk Love Songs. With Dulcimer. Boone Tolliver, BTR-22
American Folk Songs. With Dulcimer. RCA Camden, CAL 245
An Evening With John Jacob Niles. With dulcimer. Tradition Records, TLP 1036
Ballads. With dulcimer. Boone-Tolliver, BTR-23
Early American Carols and Folk Songs. With dulcimer. RCA Victor, M 718, 78 rpm
Fiftieth Anniversary Album. With dulcimer. RCA Camden, CAL - 330
I Wonder As I Wonder. With dulcimer. Tradition Records, TLP - 1023. 1957
The Seven Joys of Mary. With dulcimer. Disc no. 732, 78 rpm. 1946
Pearse, John. Recorded dulcimer selections for Da Camera Song Records, Pye Records, and Xtra Records. No other information available
Pentangle *Solomon's Seal.* Reprise, 2100
Cruel Sister. Reprise, 6430
Proffitt, Frank *Frank Proffitt.* Folkways, 3360
Frank Proffitt. Folk Legacy, 1
Frank Proffitt Memorial Album. With dulcimer, banjo. Folk Legacy Records, FSA-36. 1968
Frank Proffitt Sings Folk Songs. With dulcimer, banjo. Folkways Americana Series, 2360
Ritchie, Edna *Edna Ritchie, Viper, Kentucky.* With dulcimer. Folk Legacy Records, FSA-3
Ritchie, Jean *American Folk Tales and Songs.* Dulcimer and guitar. Tradition Records, TLP 1011. 1956
Appalachian Dulcimer. Instruction record to accompany *The Dulcimer Book,* record and book may be bought separately. Folkways, FI 8352. 1963
Appalachian Mountain Songs. Dulcimer and guitar. His Master's Voice, two record set, 10 inch discs, 78 rpm
A Time for Singing. Dulcimer, banjo, guitar, fiddle, bass, harmonica. Warner Brothers, WS 1592. 1965
Best of Jean Ritchie. Dulcimer with guitar. Prestige International, FI 14009. 1962
British Traditional Ballads in the Southern Mountains. Two record set, Folkways, FA 2301, FA 2302. 1961
Carols of All Seasons. Dulcimer, recorder, harpsichord. Tradition Records, TLP 1031. 1959
Children's Songs and Games from the Southern Appalachians. Dulcimer, guitar. Folkways, FC 7054, ten inch disc. 1957
Clear Waters Remembered. Dulcimer, guitar, fiddle, bass, banjo. Sire Records, SES 97014
Courting and Riddle Songs. (Reissue of Riverside, RLP 12 - 646, *Riddle Me This*) Washington Records, WLP 706. 1959
Courting Songs. Dulcimer and guitar. Elektra-Stratford, ELK - 22, ten inch disc. 1954
Jean Ritchie. Electra, 122. 1957
Jean Ritchie and Doc Watson at Folk City. Dulcimer, guitar, banjo, fiddle. Folkways, FA 2426. 1963
Jean Ritchie at Home. Dulcimer, banjo, guitar, fiddle, recorder. Pacifica Cascades Records.
Jean Ritchie Field Trip. With dulcimer. Collector Limited Edition, CLE 1201. 1956
Jean Ritchie Sings Traditional Mountain Songs of Her Kentucky Mountain Home. Dulcimer, guitar. Elektra-Stratford, EKS 2, ten inch disc. 1952
Kentucky Mountain Songs. Dulcimer, guitar. Elektra-Stratford, EKL-25, ten inch disc. 1954

Marching Across Green Grass. Asch, 752
Precious Memories. Dulcimer, banjo, fiddle, organ. Folkways, FA 2427. 1962
Riddle Me This. Dulcimer, banjo, guitar. Riverside, RLP 12 - 646. 1957
Ritchie Family of Kentucky. Folkways, FA 2316. 1957
Saturday Night and Sunday Too. Dulcimer, guitar, banjo, fiddle. Riverside, RLP 12 - 620. 1956
Shivaree. Dulcimer, guitar, mandolin, banjo. Esoteric Records, ES 538, ten inch disc. 1955
Singing Family of the Cumberlands. With dulcimer and guitar. Riverside, RLP 12 - 653. 1957
Songs From Kentucky. Dulcimer, guitar. Argo, ARL 1012
Rolling Stones *Aftermath.* London, 476
Ross, Claire and Hinchcliff, Pauline *All In the Morning, Folk Carols of Britain and America.* Dulcimer and guitar. Keepoint Recording Service, MF 12101
Roth, Kevin *Kevin Roth Sings and Plays Dulcimer.* With dulcimer. Folkways, FA 2367. 1974
Russell Family *The Russell Family.* Country, 734
Schilling, Jean *Old Traditions.* Traditional, 5117
Porches of the Poor. Traditional, JLS 617
Seeger, Peggy *Peggy Seeger Alone.* Argo, ZDA 81
Seeger, Peggy and Mike *Peggy N' Mike.* Argo, ZDA 80
Seeger, Peggy and MacColl, Ewan *At the Present Moment.* Rounder, 4003
Folkways Record of Contemporary Songs. Folkways, 8736
The Long Harvest. Argo, ZDA 66
The Long Harvest, Vol. Nine. Argo, ZDA 74
The Long Harvest, Vol. Ten. Argo, ZDA 75
Manchester Angel. Tradition, 2059
The Paper Stage. Argo, ZDA 99
Seeger, Peggy and Paley, Tom *Tom Paley and Peggy Seeger.* Electra, 7295
Simmons Family *The Simmons Family.* Dulcimer, autoharp, guitar. Rodney Peppenhorst Productions
Stone County Dulcimer. Dulcimer, guitar. Rodney Peppenhorst Productions
Wandering Through the Rakensack. Dulcimer, guitar, autoharp. Rodney Peppenhorst Productions, V-3053
Smith, Ralph Lee *Archive of Folk Music.* Everest, FS 204. 1963
Old Fashioned Music, Played and Sung by the Yankee Carpetbaggers. Union, 1362
Smith, Ralph Lee and Hollwell, Mary *Dulcimer Old Time and Traditional Music.* Skyline, DD 102
Southern Michigan String Band *Transplanted Old Timey Music.* Pine Tree, 509
Sturgill, Virgil *Southern Mountain Folk Songs and Ballads.* Six dulcimer selections. Riverside, RLP 12-617
Sweet Corn *All Around the Mountain.* No other information available
Summers, Andrew Rowen *Andrew Rowen Summers.* Dulcimer. Folkways, FA 2348, ten inch disc. 1957
Christmas Carols. Dulcimer Folkways, FA 2002, ten inch disc. 1956
False Ladye. Dulcimer. Folkways, FA 2044, ten inch disc. 1954
Hymns and Carols. Dulcimer. Folkways, FA 2361, ten inch disc
The Lady Gay. Dulcimer. Folkways, FA 2041, ten inch disc. 1954
Seeds of Love. Dulcimer. Folkways, 2021, ten inch disc. 1961
Unquiet Grave. Dulcimer accompaniment. Folkways, FA 2364, ten inch disc. 1954
Winston, Nat T. *Learn to Play the Dulcimer.* Instruction record, 45 rpm. Don Sellers Inc. 1969

Festivals and Miscellaneous Albums

Alabama Folk Music. Huntsville Association of Folk Music. No other information available
All Those People, Fox Hollow 1968. One dulcimer selection. Fox Hollow Records
American Folk Song Festival. Two songs with dulcimer. Folkways, FA 2358
And Not One Police, Fox Hollow 1969. Fox Hollow Records.
Berkeley Farms, Country Music From Berkeley, California. Dulcimer and other instruments. Folkways, FA 2436. 1973
Beech Mountain, North Carolina Volume II. Four dulcimer selections. Folk Legacy Records. 1965
Bury Me Beneath the Willow. Dulcimer, guitar, banjo, and harmonica. Washington Records, WLP 734
Down Came the Water, Volume II, Fox Hollow 1967. Fox Hollow Records.
Five Days Singing Volume I. Folk Legacy Records, 41
Five Days Singing Volume II. Folk Legacy Records, 42
Folk Box. Two selections with dulcimer. Electra in cooperation with Folkways, ELK-BOX. 1964
Folk Festival at Newport. Four dulcimer selections. Vanguard, VRS 9064
Folk Festival of the Smokies. Traditional Records, 528
Folk Festival of the Smokies II. Traditional Records, FFS 529
Fox Hollow 1972, Volume VII. Fox Hollow Records
Golden Ring. Dulcimer and other instruments. Folk Legacy Records, 16
Greatest Folksingers of the Sixties. Vanguard, 1718
Instrumental Music of the Southern Appalachians. Mrs. Ed Presnell plays three dulcimer selections. Tradition, TLP 1007. 1956
New Golden Ring—Five Days Singing. Twenty-six dulcimer players, Appalachian and hammered. Folk Legacy Records
Pleasant and Delightful, Volume I. Three dulcimer selections. Living Folk Records
The Rain Come Doon, Volume I, 1967 Fox Hollow Festival. Two dulcimer selections. Fox Hollow Records
The Rackensack. Rackensack Folklore Society of Mountain View, Arkansas
Traditional Music at Newport 1964, Part 2. Two dulcimer selections. Vanguard, VRS-9183
Traditional Music of Beech Mountain North Carolina. Folk Legacy Records, 22
Waterloo Peterloo. Argo, ZDA 86
World Festival of Folk Song and Dance, Biarritz—Pamplona, 1953. Two selections on the dulcimer. Westminster, WL 5334

Record Company Addresses

Most of the records listed in the discography will not be available from a local record store. It is possible to order records directly from many companies. The addresses of smaller record companies whose records were listed in the discography are provided here.

ALP, All Platinum, 96 West St., Englewood, N.J. 07631
Archive of Folk Music, C/O Everest Enterprises, 10920 Wilshire Blvd., West Los Angeles, Cal. 90024
Argo Records, C/O McGraw-Hill Records, 330 West 42nd St., New York, New York 10036
ASCH, C/O Folkways Records, 43 West 61 St., N.Y., N.Y. 10036
B & C Records, Soho Square, London W1V 5DG, England
Biograph Records, 16 River St., Chatham, N.Y. 12037
Country Records, 307 East 37th St., N.Y., N.Y. 10016
Don Sellers Inc., Box 4185, Chattanooga, Tennessee 37405
Esoteric, C/O Counterpoint Records, 815 Broadway, New York 3, New York 14904
Everest Records, Everest Enterprises, 10920 Wilshire Blvd., West Los Angeles, Cal. 90024
Folk Heritage Records, C/O Doctor Gainer, W. Va. University, Parkersburg, W. Va. 26101
Folk Legacy Records, Sharon, Conn. 06069
Folkways Records, 43 West 61 St., N.Y., N.Y. 10036
Fox Hollow Records, R.D. 1, Petersburg, New York 12138
Frailing Records, P.O. Box 14592, Gainesville, Florida 32604
Front Hall, R.D. 1, Wormer Road, Voorheesville, N.Y. 12186
His Masters Voice, London, England
Joan Lowe Enterprises, see Pacifica Cascades Records
Judson Records, C/O Riverside Records, 235 West 46th St., New York 36, New York 11361
Keepoint Recording Co., London, England
Lemco, C/O King Bluegrass, 4766 Glendale-Milford Road, Cincinnati, Ohio 45242
Library of Congress, Music Division, Recorded Sound Section, Washington, D.C. 20540
Living Folk Records, 65 Mt. Auburn St., Cambridge, Mass. 02138
Meadowlands Records, 2301 Loring Place, Bronx, N.Y. 10468
Minstrel Records, Collegium Sound Systems, 35-41 72nd St., Jackson Heights, N.Y. 11372
Pacifica Cascades Records, C/O Joan Lowe, Vida, Oregon 97488
Philo Records, The Barn, North Ferrisburg, Vermont 05473
Pine Tree Records, Marvin C. Davies, Route 5, Connersville, Indiana 47331
Prestige Records, C/O Fantasy Records, 1 Gulf and Western Plaza, N.Y., N.Y. 10023
Pye Records, 17 Great Cumberland Place, London 1WH 8AA, England
Riverside Records, 553 West 51st St., N.Y., N.Y. 14304
Rodney Pepenhorst Productions, P.O. Box 11211, Memphis, Tenn. 38111
Rounder Records, 186 West Willow Ave., Somerville, Mass. 02144
Sire Records, 165 West 74th St., N.Y., N.Y. 10023
Skyline Records, Stephens City, Virginia 22655
Tennvale Records, P.O. Box 474, Somerville, Mass. 02143
Tradition Records, C/O Everest Records, 10920 Wilshire Blvd., West Los Angeles, Cal. 90024
Traditional Records, P.O. Box 8, Cosby, Tenn. 37722
Trailer Records, 5 North Villas, London N.W. 1, England
Vibrant Records, Route 2, Talbott, Tenn. 37877
Washington Records, 235 West 46th St., New York 36, N.Y. 11203
Westminster Records, C/O ABC Records, 8255 Beverly Blvd., Los Angeles, Cal. 90048
Xtra Records, C/O Transatlantic Records, 86 Marlebone High St., London, W1M 4AY, England

Unidentified dulcimer player, circa 1930